Transpacific Displacement

Transpacific Displacement

*Ethnography, Translation, and Intertextual Travel
in Twentieth-Century American Literature*

Yunte Huang

UNIVERSITY OF CALIFORNIA PRESS

Berkeley   Los Angeles   London

University of California Press
Berkeley and Los Angeles, California

University of California Press, Ltd.
London, England

Sections of this book were presented at the following conferences: Conference on Contemporary Poetry, Cornell University, 1995; Conference on American and Russian Literatures, Stevens Institute of Technology, New Jersey, 1996; Twentieth-Century Literature Conference, University of Louisville, Kentucky, 1997; Cross-Cultural Poetics Conference, University of Minnesota, Minneapolis, 1997; The New Modernisms Conference, Pennsylvania State University, State College, 1999; and Bilingual Aesthetics Conference in 1999, English Department Seminar in 2000, and Asian Cultural Studies Seminar in 2000, all at Harvard. I am grateful to the editors of the following journals where portions of this book appeared earlier, in different forms: *River City* 16:1 (1996) and *Hopscotch* 2:4 (2001).

Grateful acknowledgment is given to New Directions Publishing Corporation and Faber and Faber Ltd. for permission to quote extensively from the following copyrighted works by Ezra Pound: *The Cantos* (Copyright © 1934, 1937, 1940, 1948, 1956, 1959, 1962, 1963, 1966, and 1968 by Ezra Pound); *Guide to Kulchur* (Copyright © 1970 by Ezra Pound); *Personae* (Copyright © 1926 by Ezra Pound); *Selected Letters 1907–1941* (Copyright © 1950 by Ezra Pound). Previously unpublished material by Ezra Pound (Copyright © by Mary de Rachewiltz and Omar S. Pound) is used by permission of New Directions Publishing Corporation agents. I thank City Lights Books for permission to reprint from Ernest Fenollosa, *The Chinese Written Character as a Medium for Poetry* (Copyright © 1936 by Ezra Pound). I also thank Cornell University Press for permission to reprint from Naoki Sakai, *Voices of the Past: The Status of Language in Eighteenth-Century Japanese Discourse* (Copyright © 1991 by Cornell University). Grateful acknowledgment is made to New Directions Publishing Corporation for permission to reprint poems by Bei Dao, from *The August Sleepwalker* (Copyright © 1988 by Bei Dao; translation copyright © 1988 by Bonnie McDougall) and *Forms of Distance* (Copyright ©1993 by Bei Dao; translation copyright © 1994 by David Hinton); and to the Harvard University Press for permission to reprint from Ezra Pound, *Shih-Ching: The Classical Anthology Defined by Confucius* (Copyright © 1954, 1982 by the President and Fellows of Harvard College).

Library of Congress Cataloging-in-Publication Data

Huang, Yunte.
    Transpacific displacement : ethnography, translation, and intertextual travel in twentieth-century American literature / Yunte Huang.
        p.   cm.
    Includes bibliographical references and index.
    ISBN 0–520–22886–3 (cloth : alk. paper).—ISBN 0–520–23223–2 (pbk. : alk. paper)
        1. American literature—Chinese American authors—History and criticism.   2. American literature—20th century—History and criticism.   3. Chinese literature—Appreciation—United States.   4. American literature—Chinese influences.   5. Chinese Americans—Intellectual life.   6. Chinese Americans in mass media.   7. Chinese Americans in literature.   8. Immigrants in literature.   9. Ethnology in literature.   10. Intertextuality.   I. Title.

PS153.C45 H83   2002
810.9′005—dc21   2001027241

Manufactured in the United States of America
10   09   08   07   06   05   04   03
10   9   8   7   6   5   4   3   2   1

The paper used in this publication meets the minimum requirements of ANSI/NISO Z39.48–1992 (R 1997) (Permanence of Paper). ♾

For

HANK LAZER

*my guide, my tourist, and
my fellow traveler*

Indeed, is it not the chief value of travel, and of studying history and alien literature, that it lifts the veil of our own, necessarily narrow, local and racial consciousness, and reveals to us over and over a broader human horizon?

Ernest Fenollosa, "Notes for a
General Article on Chinese Poetry"

CONTENTS

ILLUSTRATIONS

ACKNOWLEDGMENTS

A study of transpacific migrations of cultural meanings, this book is also a record of my own peregrinations along the same routes and a testimony of my intellectual debts to the many people whose names I cannot possibly all list here. I would, however, like to express my enormous gratitude to Charles Bernstein and Dennis Tedlock, my two mentors at SUNY-Buffalo's Poetics Program, who taught me the value of poetry as cultural and cross-cultural criticism. Bernstein's wit and humor and Tedlock's personal generosity and intellectual depth made the interminable bitter winters of Buffalo magical seasons of inspiration. I also wish to thank Robert Creeley and Susan Howe, whose devotion to innovative poetry has had a sustained influence on me. Thanks should also go to Rodolphe Gasché, whose remarkable clarity in thinking has helped me rethink my project. The publication of this book would not have been possible without the enthusiastic support of Marjorie Perloff and Leo Ou-fan Lee. Over the years I have benefited greatly from Perloff's kind encouragement and superb advice. Similarly, Lee has been very generous in providing both personal friendship and intellectual companionship since I had the fortune to become his colleague at Harvard in 1999.

Among the people who read the manuscript in its various stages, I especially want to thank Larry Buell, my departmental chair and senior colleague, who reviewed the entire manuscript with meticulous care and gave me extremely valuable advice on revisions. I also owe enormous debts to the following colleagues at Harvard, who by either verbal or written comments left their mark on this book: Stephen Greenblatt, Marc Shell, Werner Sollors, Sacvan Bercovitch, Marjorie Garber, Helen Vendler, Philip Fisher, Elisa New, Forrest Gander, and Bob Kiely. I feel particularly privileged to be in the company of the following junior colleagues—a group of first year "garden-level" residents of the Barker Center and a "cohort" of brilliant and exciting young scholars—who provided me with much-needed moral support and intellectual insights: Lynn Festa, Oren Izenberg, Ann Rowland, and Sharmila Sen. Some Harvard colleagues outside the English Department, especially Doris Sommer, Stephen Owen, and Sophie Xiaofei Tian, generously shared their expertise on the subject. Thanks should also go to the following friends, professors, and colleagues, who supported me in various ways: Robert Bertholf, Michael Basinski, Sue Michel, Barbara Tedlock, James Sherry, Joel Kuszai, Mike Kelleher, Ben Friedlander, Eleni Stecopoulous, Seunghyeok Kweon, Jina Kim, Neil Schmitz, Victor Doyno, Peter Logan, Catherine Davies, Elizabeth Meese, John Yau, Fred Wah, Zhang Ziqing, and Sui Xin.

My whole career in the United States would not even have begun without the support, guidance, friendship, and love of the person to whom this book is dedicated. Hank Lazer sustained me during my most difficult years surviving in the South. He has helped me and seen me grow in the past nine years as both a person and a scholar living and writing in a language and culture not my own. He has been my best and most generous reader, always ready to offer insights and advice. Whatever I have achieved today is owed in no small part to him. I also wish to thank my editor at the University of California Press, Linda Norton, for her unfailing faith in this book and for her superb editorial guidance; while the first factor made the task of manuscript preparation conversely more challenging, the second made it much more reassuring. Thanks should also go to Mary Koon and Caralyn Bialo of the same press, Declan Spring of New Directions Publishing Corporation, and Alfred Mueller of the Beinecke Library at Yale for their very able assistance, and to Ellen Browning for her excellent copyediting work.

Last but by no means least, I remain grateful to my wife Tsen-Chen (Julia) Hsiao for her love, support, patience, and impatience over the years, and to our daughter Isabelle, whose miraculous arrival in 2000 has brought wonder to our life and who kept me up every night to cuddle her while finishing this book.

Introduction

When I was growing up in a small town in southern China, I had a next-door neighbor who was old and blind. As the story goes, he was born in that same house next to mine. At the age of two, he lost his vision as a result of an illness. At seven, he was sent to *Meiguo* (America; literally, the "beautiful country") to live with his relatives there. He learned the English language and later pursued a career as an interpreter. After retiring, he moved back to our town and planned to live there for the remainder of his life.

As a child, I was fascinated by this question: "What does he know about Meiguo since he hasn't really *seen* it?" I often imagined myself putting this question to him and wondered how he would respond. In childish vagaries, I convinced myself that whatever the old man might tell me would literally be hearsay, because it would not be as real as the way I saw, for instance, the bright golden sun, of which, I had heard, he had only some vague visual memories. But I never had the chance to ask him any questions. In fact, I never even saw him with my own eyes. He was too old to go out and would meet no one except those who went to his house for English lessons. I knew of him only by overhearing adults' conversations and the gossip told by my sister, who had a friend who took English lessons from him. In this sense, my present account of him is as much hearsay as I thought his account of Meiguo would have been.

I begin with this anecdote of a "blind" traveler because this book is about travelers and their ways of seeing, knowing, and telling. Moreover, the travelers to be considered here manifest "extraordinary" ways of seeing, knowing, and telling, ways that are often deemed inauthentic. Their writings have seldom been read the way *The Travels of Marco Polo* or *Mandeville's Travels* have been read: as travel narratives, as accounts "of the various races of mankind and of the diversities of the sundry regions of the World."[1] My naive "I," who dismissed the old blind man as an unreliable seer, would agree with those who refuse to see these writings as travel narratives, because that "I" would insist that many of these writers haven't really seen those places or cultures they describe. The naiveté of this notion was revealed to me only when I myself became a traveler as well as an avid reader of travelogues. Especially since I came to the United States, the great distance from "home" has enabled me to think of that old familiar space from an increasingly defamiliarized perspective and kindled in me a strong urge to maintain connections by writing and reading: writing letters to friends and family, receiving letters from them, and looking for all sorts of travel narratives or ethnographic accounts about China. Within the last category, one kind of text has particularly fascinated me because it reminds me time and again of my old "blind" neighbor: it is the kind that is never directly about China as a geographical space but rather about China from the perspectives of language and literature. I don't mean that these are just books about Chinese language or literature per se; instead, they approach the "folk-mind" of China by means of its language and literature. It is true that the authors of these texts may or may not have lived in the culture they describe, and it is also true that, as a result, very few of these texts have even been read as travel narratives or ethnographies. But, as I have slowly come to realize, these authors, just like my old neighbor, do travel and see—only differently. And for me to deny the fruits of their travels and ethnographies is to commit recidivism.

1. Marco Polo, *The Book of Marco Polo, the Venetian: Concerning the Kingdoms and Marvels of the East*, trans. and ed. Colonel Henry Yule (London: John Murray, 1871), 1.

Now these authors and their texts have made their way into my book. It is my intention to show that we all travel in the world of texts. Even when we arrive physically at a new place, our "bookish" preconceptions always interact with, if not simply predetermine, what we see and how we see it. What I call *transpacific displacement* is a historical process of textual migration of cultural meanings, meanings that include linguistic traits, poetics, philosophical ideas, myths, stories, and so on. And such displacement is driven in particular by the writers' desire to appropriate, capture, mimic, parody, or revise the Other's signifying practices in an effort to describe the Other. In my study, these strategies of linguistic appropriations share features with, but ultimately depart from, what Stephen Greenblatt has called "appropriative mimesis." In his remarkable study of the European encounters with the New World, Greenblatt identifies a cross-cultural strategy for linguistic acquisition—"appropriative mimesis," which he defines as "imitation in the interest of acquisition," imitation that "need not have entailed any grasp of the cultural reality of the other, only a willingness to make contact and to effect some kind of exchange."[2] By contrast, in my study I want to emphasize that the appropriation of the Chinese language in Imagism and other cases is made not merely to possess "a token of otherness," but also to grasp a cultural reality identifiable in linguistic patterns. That is, whereas the European imitators in Greenblatt's case were not interested in the cultural reality of the Other as such, the authors I study could not avoid creating ethnographic images of the Other. Better still, cultural descriptions often lie at the heart of their work.

In my study, there are three textual means by which the imaging of the Other's cultural reality may be attempted: ethnography, translation, and intertextual travel. The definition of ethnography is revealed by its etymology: the writing (*-graphy*) of culture (*ethno-*). I concur with some theoretical articulations in the anthropology of the past decade or so

2. Stephen J. Greenblatt, *Marvelous Possessions: The Wonder of the New World* (Chicago: University of Chicago Press, 1991), 99.

that propose to foreground the textual nature of what is usually understood as positivist, social-science work. I suggest that ethnography, a hybrid genre of literature and anthropology, is often produced by the intertextual tactics of absorbing other texts and transforming them into an account that fulfills the ethnographer's preconceptions of a culture.

Similarly, translation involves not a transportation of meaning from an originality to its equivalent in another language but a process in which multiple readings of the "original" are reduced to a version that foregrounds the translator's own agenda. Just as the ethnographer invents a culture with intertextual tactics, the translator creates the "original" from a textualization that is often invisible to the reader. The illusion of the "original" corresponds to that of a "place" that a traveler is supposed to have seen and to report upon.

Intertextual travel, which to some extent overlaps the concepts of ethnography and translation, describes one of the primary modes by which we humans see any part of the world without really being there. As Lao Tzu said almost three thousand years ago, "Without going beyond the door, one knows the world; without peering out the window, one knows the way of heaven." Yet, it is not the way of heaven that we are seeking but merely the intertextual trajectories of getting to know the world. For such a world is, as Paul Ricoeur suggests, "the ensemble of references opened up by the texts."[3] From all those new or dusty volumes, we read and glean things about places and people we have never seen. We travel from one text to another, from one version to another, to compile our own text or version, to create our own travelogue.

These three concepts—ethnography, translation, and intertextual travel—will accompany us on the journey to investigate transpacific migrations of cultural meanings. I illustrate the ways in which America's imaging of Asia over the last century has been successful, or not, through these three trajectories. Imagism, for example, creates an ethnography that takes Ori-

---

3. Paul Ricoeur, *Interpretation Theory: Discourse and the Surplus of Meaning* (Fort Worth: Texas Christian University Press, 1976), 36.

ental linguistic traits as its central concern and produces a translation that refashions an "image" of Chinese/Japanese poetry. And both the ethnography and translation depend in turn on intertextual maneuvers, such as generalizing specific terms, retouching earlier translations, or even manufacturing examples. Or, in Maxine Hong Kingston's work, the making of an "American" myth is achieved by means of textual translation: Kingston fills in the fractures between source materials and her text and erases the linguistic foreignness embodied by *intertexts*. Or, America's cultural description of contemporary China is showcased in the translations of Chinese poetry. Many translators are in effect engaged in producing ethnographies, because their textual renderings are often (mis)guided by (pre)conceptions of China's political reality but overlook the cultural materiality embodied in the very poems they are translating.

This book necessarily entails a critique of the truth claims made by some of the travelers. Ezra Pound's intertextual invention of *Kulchur*, for instance, will necessarily fall apart as his pancultural scheme can no longer hold together the "complex, polyvocal textuality" of his work created by "using ideological swatches from many social and historical sectors of his own society and an immense variety of other cultures."[4] Likewise, the textual fractures in Kingston's work will haunt her realist claims, and the formal innovations of Chinese poetry will forestall American translators' preconceptions of contemporary China.

Yet, the journey that I have undertaken does not end with an evaluation of the success or failure, validity or invalidity of these "extraordinary" travelogues. What I hope will emerge eventually from this study is an articulation of an American literature that transcends cultural and linguistic boundaries, a national literature rooted in transnationalism and committed to translingual practices, of which ethnography, translation, and intertextual travel are salient examples. To argue for such a literature is to argue against some nativist trends in literary studies that seek to construct a history of American literature deprived of its transnational

4. Charles Bernstein, *A Poetics* (Cambridge: Harvard University Press, 1992), 123.

character. It is also to argue against both assimilationist and segregation-ist models of ethnic or, more specifically, Asian American literature that make Americanization their goal and discount the vitality of otherness.

Let me try to be clear: On the one hand, I want to use transpacific displacement as a model for critiqing the somewhat complacent, self-sufficient world of "American" literature and to cast into relief the significance of America's "experience of the foreign"[5] to the construc-tion of its cultural identity. The transnational migration of cultural meanings by way of ethnography, translation, and intertextual travel is intrinsic and vital to the formation (and possibly, deformation or desta-bilization) of any national literature. The transpacific routes I am trying to open up for American literature, while they parallel in spirit the transatlantic diaspora,[6] are meant to articulate the particularity and significance of America's Asian Pacific experience in the past century or so. On the other hand, the history of transpacific displacement, espe-cially the history of *textual migration*, which involves not just exercising Orientalist fantasies but also acquiring actual knowledge of the Other, including appropriating or mimicking the Other's ways of speaking, writing, seeing, and knowing, will provide the most meaningful back-ground for the deepening and expansion of Asian American literature. Placed in the larger perspective of transpacific displacement, which is, as I argue, indispensable to the creation of American literature, Asian American literature will be able to maintain its subversive role in under-mining the "American" canon without risking the danger of segregating itself. When the so-called minor is recognized as vital to the formation

5. I borrow this expression from Antoine Berman, who, in *The Experience of the For-eign: Culture and Translation in Romantic Germany* (trans. S. Heyvaert [Albany: State Uni-versity of New York Press, 1992]), suggests that the *Bildung* of German national culture was contingent on a strategy of translation, allowing the Other to enter the body of self.

6. The works in this field are too numerous for me to provide a comprehensive list, but several have stood out among others: Greenblatt, *Marvelous Possessions;* Henry Louis Gates Jr., *The Signifying Monkey: A Theory of African-American Literary Criticism* (New York: Oxford University Press, 1988); and Paul Gilroy, *The Black Atlantic: Modernity and Double Consciousness* (Cambridge: Harvard University Press, 1993).

of the major, it can no longer be segregated and the polarity of minor versus major is destabilized. Here I am fortunate to be in the company of a number of scholars who have argued eloquently for the vital significance of America's transpacific experience. Lisa Lowe, for instance, opens her powerful critique of the institution of citizenship by positing that "understanding Asian immigration to the United States is fundamental to understanding the racialized foundations of both the emergence of the United States as a nation and the development of American capitalism."[7] David Palumbo-Liu also maintains that "the formation of 'modern America' in the early twentieth century is so deeply and particularly attached to the Pacific region [that] managing the modern was inseparable from managing Asian America."[8] And Rob Wilson, in his most recent study of the American Pacific, creates a new "U.S. field imaginary" by resettling the wilderness of American literary history in the South Pacific and beyond.[9] But in ways I shall explain later in this introduction, my project focuses on a different, although not separate, aspect of the transpacific.

■ ■ ■

> The analysis of dialects enables us to follow the history of words and of concepts through long periods of time and over distant areas. The introduction of new inventions and migration into distant countries are often indicated by the appearance of new words the origins of which may be ascertained. Thus the history of language reflects the history of culture.
>
> *Franz Boas, "The Aims of Ethnology" (1888)*

7. Lisa Lowe, *Immigrant Acts: On Asian American Cultural Politics* (Durham: Duke University Press, 1996), ix.

8. David Palumbo-Liu, *Asian/American: Historical Crossings of a Racial Frontier* (Stanford: Stanford University Press, 1999), 17.

9. Rob Wilson, *Reimagining the American Pacific: From South Pacific to Bamboo Ridge and Beyond* (Durham: Duke University Press, 2000).

One crucial theoretical inspiration for my project is Boasian cultural and linguistic anthropology. Around the turn of the century, the German Jewish anthropologist Franz Boas and his followers actively engaged in reshaping America's racial discourse by repudiating eugenics and other forms of racism based on nineteenth-century biological evolutionism and by moving the focus of anthropology from sheerly physical studies to a recognition of "the importance of language as a factor in the study of culture."[10] Among Boas's voluminous writings, no piece articulates his position on the issue of language and anthropology better than his long introduction to the *Handbook of American Indian Languages* (1911). Published by the Bureau of American Ethnology as Bulletin 40, the handbook was intended to classify the American languages, document "the essential features of the morphology and phonetics," and set forth their "essential psychological characteristics."[11] As head of the project, Boas wrote an introduction to the handbook, in which he presented a comprehensive view of the relationships among three concepts that would loom conspicuously in twentieth-century thinking: race, language, and culture.

Writing at a time when evolutionist biologism was fortifying its grip on social theories, Boas made a radical move by emphasizing the *artificial* character of the concepts used in anthropology (the *science* of humankind): "We recognize thus that every classification of mankind must be more or less artificial, according to the point of view selected" (14). He doubted that among the key concepts—race, language, and culture—there is any intrinsic, biological tie binding them together: "The probabilities are decidedly in favor of the assumption that there is no necessity to assume that originally each language and culture were confined to a single type, or that each type and culture were confined to one language: in short, that there has been at any time a close correlation between these three phenomena" (13). To suspend the tie between

10. Melville J. Herskovits, *Franz Boas: The Science of Man in the Making* (New York: Charles Scribner's Sons, 1953), 7.

11. Franz Boas, ed., *Handbook of American Indian Languages* (Washington: Government Printing Office, 1911), v.

race, language, and culture was, at that time, to expel the popular colonialist notion according to which linguistic "primitiveness" always correlated with barbarity and racial inferiority.

Having undercut physiologism's dominance in the newly founded discipline, Boas went on to foreground the significance of language to the study of humankind. In the section entitled "Linguistics and Ethnology," he gives two reasons that the study of language should occupy a primary rather than subordinate position in the discipline. The first, practical reason is rather simple: Not knowing the natives' language greatly handicaps an ethnographer's work. Relying on native interpreters, as most ethnographers do, is not a good solution because interpreters often interfere with the communication between ethnographers and native informants by inserting their own interpretations.

The second, theoretical reason is fundamental: "The purely linguistic inquiry is part and parcel of a thorough investigation of the psychology of the peoples of the world. If ethnology is understood as the science dealing with the mental phenomena of the life of the peoples of the world, *human language, one of the most important manifestations of mental life, would seem to belong naturally to the field of work of ethnology*" (63; emphasis added). Moreover, Boas maintains that whereas other ethnological phenomena, such as social customs, often rise into consciousness and easily subject themselves to reinterpretation, linguistic phenomena seldom rise into consciousness and hence their formation can be studied directly without "the misleading and disturbing factors of secondary explanations, which are so common in ethnology, so much so that they generally obscure the real history of the development of ideas entirely" (71). Summarizing this crucial section of the introduction, Boas writes:

> Thus it appears that from practical, as well as from theoretical,
> points of view, the study of language must be considered as one of
> the most important branches of ethnological study, because, on the
> one hand, a thorough insight into ethnology can not be gained without practical knowledge of language, and, on the other hand, the
> fundamental concepts illustrated by human languages are not dis-

tinct in kind from ethnological phenomena; and because, furthermore, the peculiar characteristics of languages are clearly reflected
in the views and customs of the peoples of the world. (73)

Here lies the Boasian legacy, what Dennis Tedlock and Bruce Mannheim
have called "the cachet of Boasian cultural and linguistic anthropology,"
that is, "in identifying forms of patterning specific to language and culture (and to *a* language and *a* culture), irreducible to physiology" (10).
Such a lucid articulation for the fundamental value of language, especially of the Other's language, in the study of humankind has inspired
generations of anthropologists departing for the field not only to observe
nonverbal social acts but also to document speech events and collect textual data. Mary Austin's *The American Rhythm* (1923), Ruth Benedict's *Patterns of Culture* (1934), Zora Neale Hurston's *Mules and Men* (1935), and
Paul Radin's *The Culture of the Winnebago* (1947), to name just a few, are
all works that, coming directly or indirectly out of the Boasian school,
deal with cultural traits as manifested conspicuously in language.

For me to study twentieth-century America's transpacific imagination in light of Boasian linguistic and cultural anthropology is by no
means a whimsical choice. As I show in this book, not only have the
writers/ethnographers under consideration, ranging from the Imagists
to the contemporary American translators of Chinese poetry, worked in
ways that profoundly resemble Boasian anthropology, but more important, the issue of language has throughout history played a crucial role
in Western ethnographies of Asia, a role I illustrate by way of outlining
Imagism's cross-cultural genealogy.

■ ■ ■

The study of Chinese poetry is an important part of the
study of Chinese culture.

Ernest Fenollosa, field notebook entry,
October 14, 1900

The starting point of my study of twentieth-century America's transpacific experience is Imagism. In its narrow sense—as an actively promoted school of poetry, beginning with the publication of H. D.'s Imagistic poems in *Poetry* (Chicago) in late 1912 and ending with the last volume of *Some Imagist Poets: An Anthology* put out by Amy Lowell in 1917—Imagism lasted no more than five years. But in its broad sense, as a vital experiment in Anglo-American modernism, Imagism outlived this short span of time. In fact, Imagism originated from a club hangout of a group of poets in London, in 1909, led by T. E. Hulme; Imagistic poems continued to be written after 1917, and 1930 saw the publication of *Imagist Anthology*, with an introduction by Ford Madox Ford. In many of his cantos written through the late 1960s, Ezra Pound still applied Imagistic methods to his writing. Even more important, Imagism broke new ground in America's transpacific imagination and set in motion a powerful force in twentieth-century American culture that continually looked east for inspirations and alternatives, a force that has enlisted cultural icons and influential writers ranging from Jack Kerouac to Allen Ginsburg, Kenneth Rexroth, John Cage, Gary Snyder, Robert Bly, W. S. Merwin, Robert Haas, and more.

I use the term *Imagism* to refer to a whole body of writings that are in various ways associated with both the narrow and the broad senses of the term. Not only does it include Imagistic poems by Ezra Pound, Amy Lowell, H. D., Richard Aldington, John Gould Fletcher, and others who labeled themselves "Imagists," but it also refers to the large amount of work that directly gave rise to the school of Imagism: the introductory, scholarly, translational, and ethnographic work of Ernest Fenollosa, Florence Ayscough, Percival Lowell, and many others. What characterizes both groups of people is their shared interest in Oriental linguistic cultures. Together they created not only a school of poetry that advocates the famous three Imagistic principles dictated by Pound in "A Few Don'ts by an Imagiste," but also a body of ethnographic discourse that fashions an image of the Orient projected largely through linguistic traits.

Taken as a whole, Imagism was from the very beginning interlocked with centuries of Western views of the Chinese language. Since the Renaissance, European conceptions of the Chinese language oscillated between extolling it as a superior embodiment of the so-called *lingua Adamica* and condemning it as a primitive, inferior tongue. In the seventeenth century, when a number of Jesuit missionaries to China started to send back detailed reports on the culture and language they encountered, they precipitated the European search for a *lingua universalis*, which often ended up identifying Chinese as a prototype of such a language. According to David E. Mungello in *Curious Land: Jesuit Accommodation and the Origin of Sinology* (1985), the search itself was the result of the cross-fertilization of three elements: The first is a biblical belief that Adam's language was spoken by all of his descendants before the Tower of Babel; the second is a medieval idea about the art of memory that led to the attempt to establish a universal language; and the third is the seventeenth-century Scientific Revolution (175). The reports of Jesuit missionaries, with whom many key seventeenth-century European intellectuals corresponded, created a Sinophilism, because they made the Europeans believe that they had finally found in Chinese the prototypical human language, one documented by the biblical statement that begins the story of Babel: "Now the whole world had one language and a common speech" (Genesis 11:1).

In a book entitled *An Historical Essay Endeavoring a Probability That the Language of the Empire of China Is the Primitive Language* (1669), the Englishman John Webb sought to prove that Chinese was perhaps the language from which all others later sprang.[12] Webb's argument was based primarily on biblical history: He claimed that China had been peopled by descendants of Noah before the "confusion of tongues." By contrast, Francis Bacon's and Gottfried Wilhelm Leibniz's fascination with Chinese was more of a philosophical or scientific nature. Both of them believed that

---

12. Jonathan Spence, *The Chan's Great Continent: China in Western Minds* (New York: W. W. Norton, 1998), 82.

it was possible to discover Real Characters, or symbols whose representation of things and notions was natural rather than conventional (Mungello 183). A leader of the emerging Scientific Revolution, Francis Bacon (1561–1625) was dissatisfied with existing European languages and called for the development of a new universal language. Reading contemporary Jesuit writings led him to idealize Chinese characters as Real Characters: "It is the use of China, and the kingdoms of the High Levant, to write in characters real, which express neither letters nor words in gross, but things or notions; insomuch as countries and provinces, which understand not one another's language, can nevertheless read one another's writings, because the characters are accepted more generally than the languages do extend" (qtd. in Mungello, 184).

Likewise, Leibniz was also searching for what he called the Universal Characteristic. For Leibniz, such characters should be "written, drawn or engraved signs which signified not words, letters or syllables, but things and ideas" (ibid. 192). Through his long correspondence with Jesuit missionaries in China, Leibniz became increasingly fascinated by the possibility of Chinese's being an example of the ideal language. His obsession with both the Chinese language and philosophical ideas went so far that he suggested "we need missionaries from the Chinese" (Leibniz 51).

During the eighteenth century, however, European regard for the Chinese language took a nosedive, primarily because China as a nation could no longer fit into the central premise of human progress formulated by the most influential European historiographers of that century. In his *Outlines of a Philosophy of the History of Man* (1784), Johann Gottfried von Herder described the Chinese empire as "an embalmed mummy, wrapped in silk, and painted with hieroglyphics" (296). He then condemned the Chinese language as a product of what he thought to be a contemptible culture:

> What a want of invention in the great, and what miserable
> refinement in trifles, are displayed in contriving for this language,
> the vast number of eighty thousand compound characters from a few
> rude hieroglyphics, six or more different modes of writing which
> distinguish the Chinese from every other nation upon Earth. Their

pictures of monsters and dragons, their minute care in the drawing of figures without regularity, the pleasure afforded their eyes by the disorderly assemblages of their gardens, the naked greatness or minute nicety in their buildings, the vain pomp of their dress, equipage, and amusements, their lantern feasts and fire-works, their long nails and cramped feet, their barbarous train of attendants, bowings, ceremonies, distinctions, and courtesies, require a mungal [Mongol] organization. So little taste for true nature, so little feeling of internal satisfaction, beauty, and worth, prevail through all these, that a neglected mind alone could arrive at this train of political cultivation, and allow itself to be so thoroughly modelled by it. As the Chinese are immoderately fond of gilt paper and varnish, the neatly painted lines of their intricate characters, and the jingle of fine sentences; the cast of their minds resembles this varnish and gilt paper, these characters and clink of syllables. (qtd. in Spence, 99–100)

Georg Wilhelm Friedrich Hegel (1770–1831), who depended for his view of Chinese on the earlier Jesuit sources as well as on the merchant accounts of his day, decided that China should be placed outside what he envisioned to be the true march of history. As a result, the Chinese language was consigned to the realm of the symbolic, which, in Hegel's theory of art, is inferior to the classic and the romantic.

It was in nineteenth-century America that a revival of interest in the Chinese language occurred. And here, in the search for the "language of nature," is the immediate intellectual antecedent to Imagism. Indeed, when Emerson envisioned a language that is "fossil poetry," or "a poetry and philosophy of insight and not of tradition," he both revived and anticipated in some way an idealized view of the Chinese language. In addition, his philosophical thinking, as some scholars have pointed out, was very much under the influence of Chinese classics.[13] The link between the Emersonian quest and the Chinese language was borne out, as we shall

13. See Frederic Ives Carpenter, *Emerson and Asia* (Cambridge: Harvard University Press, 1930), and the more recent Arthur Versluis, *American Transcendentalism and Asian Religions* (New York: Oxford University Press, 1993).

see, by the work of Ernest Fenollosa, a New Englander and Harvard graduate steeped in Transcendental philosophy, and by the poetry and poetics of Ezra Pound, who also stood firmly in the Emersonian tradition.[14]

At the end of the nineteenth century, only a decade or so before the birth of Imagism, Otto Jespersen, a Danish linguist writing in English, published an influential book, *Progress in Language* (1894). In it, Jespersen redefines linguistic history as progressive, as opposed to decaying, and, interestingly enough, he places the Chinese language in an advanced stage of the progression. He emphasizes with capital letters: "THE EVOLUTION OF LANGUAGE SHOWS A PROGRESSIVE TENDENCY FROM INSEPARABLE IRREGULAR CONGLOMERATION TO FREELY AND REGULARLY COMBINABLE SHORT ELEMENTS" (127).

Chinese, according to Jespersen, contains these "freely and regularly combinable short elements" and should therefore be characterized as a "modern language." The attribution of modernity to Chinese would have significant implications in Imagism, which not only absorbed precursory conceptualizations of the Oriental languages, but, more important, revised them.

However, most studies of Imagism either ignore its intrinsic cross-culturalism by presenting a myopic nativist account of this exhilarating episode of America's transpacific experience or disregard the significant ethnographic aspect of Imagism, which has much larger cultural implications than the model of comparative poetics can recognize. They either conceive of Imagism as a modern revolt against the poetry of the immediate past that took place *inside* the Anglo-American literary tradition or regard it merely as an interlingual, aesthetic project devoid of ethnographic contents.[15] Arguing against both of these conceptualizations, I maintain that Imagism, born out of the encounter between the West and

14. See Cary Wolfe, *The Limits of American Literary Ideology in Pound and Emerson* (New York: Cambridge University Press, 1993); and Robert Kern, *Orientalism, Modernism, and the American Poem* (Cambridge: Cambridge University Press, 1996).

15. For works that belong to the first category, see Glenn Hughes, *Imagism and the Imagists: A Study in Modern Poetry* (New York: The Humanities Press, 1960), Stanley K.

the East, constitutes an ethnographic discourse about the Far East that was produced collectively by writers with an ethnographic bent, by ethnographers both "out there" and "here at home." I identify pairs of data collectors/writers-at-home in the history of Imagism: Ernest Fenollosa/Ezra Pound, Florence Ayscough/Amy Lowell, and Percival Lowell/Amy Lowell. By calling them field-workers or data collectors, I by no means want to devalue the works of Fenollosa, Ayscough, or P. Lowell as writers. They are ethnographers in their own right: Fenollosa produced two colossal volumes of *Epochs of Chinese and Japanese Art*, one monumental monograph on Chinese characters, to which I refer in detail, and a series of reviews on various Far Eastern subjects; Ayscough wrote significant ethnographies on China, such as *A Chinese Mirror* and *Chinese Women*; and P. Lowell published, among other works, a highly acclaimed account of Japan, *The Soul of the Far East*. By pairing these three authors (Fenollosa, Ayscough, P. Lowell) with the Imagist poets (Pound and A. Lowell) as field-workers/ethnographers-at-home, I mean to emphasize that the latter have drawn upon various ethnographic materials provided by the former through the channels of personal correspondence, collaboration, and published work.

While I find both the nativist and the traditional comparative poetic approaches to Imagism insufficient in recognizing its larger cultural framework, my interest in remapping the textual trajectories of twentieth-century America's transpacific imagination has another intellectual aspiration. As I stated earlier, in recent years there has been a plethora of studies

---

Coffman Jr., *Imagism: A Chapter for the History of Modern Poetry* (New York: Octagon Books, 1972), and J. B. Harmer, *Victory in Limbo: Imagism 1908–1917* (London: Secker & Warburg, 1975); for works that belong to the second category, see Wai-Lim Yip, *Ezra Pound's Cathay* (Princeton: Princeton University Press, 1969), Hugh Kenner, *The Pound Era* (Berkeley and Los Angeles: University of California Press, 1971), Beongcheon Yu, *The Great Circle: American Writers and the Orient* (Detroit: Wayne State University Press, 1983), Sanehide Kodama, *American Poetry and Japanese Culture* (Hamden, Conn.: Archon Books, 1984), and Zhaoming Qian, *Orientalism and Modernism* (Durham: Duke University Press, 1995).

on the cultural politics of the transpacific. To name only a few such studies: Lisa Lowe (1996), David Palumbo-Liu (1999), Aihwa Ong (1999), Rey Chow (1993), Arif Dirlik (1993), and Rob Wilson (2000). However, it will not escape any concerned reader that few of these very important studies have engaged closely with what I shall characterize as *textual migrations of cultural meanings*. Such a phrase may sound tautological, for how else can cultural meanings migrate if not textually or discursively? But the deceptive appearance of tautology, the need to re-emphasize, reveals precisely the lack of attention to textuality and its vibrant history in current transpacific studies as well as in American literary studies as a whole.

One day when I was doing research on Pound's and Fenollosa's manuscripts at the Beinecke Library at Yale, I came across a handwritten draft of the latter's well-known essay, "The Chinese Written Language as a Medium for Poetry."[16] As the title indicates, this is one of the earlier drafts of Fenollosa's monograph on Chinese written characters, which was later edited and promoted by Ezra Pound, making it a landmark of American modernism.[17] The first and the fourth passages in the draft are almost identical to the ones in the published version—Fenollosa opens with a call for the deepening of transpacific understanding (see figs. 1 and 2):

> This twentieth century not only turns a new page in the book of the world, but opens another and a startling chapter. Vistas of strange futures unfold for man, of world-embracing cultures half-weaned from Europe, of hitherto undreamed responsibilities for nations and races. . . .

16. See the Beinecke Collection, YCAL MSS 43, B101 F4248. Fenollosa's manuscript is now part of the Ezra Pound Collection in the Beinecke Rare Book and Manuscript Library at Yale University. The manuscript is numbered according to boxes and folders under the call number YCAL MSS 43. The Fenollosa part runs from Folder 4211 in Box 98 to Folder 4282 in Box 103. Hereafter, I will follow this numbering practice when discussing Fenollosa's and Pound's manuscripts.

17. The monograph was written sometime after Fenollosa returned from Japan in 1901 and before his sudden death in 1908. It was then edited by Ezra Pound and published first in four installments in *The Little Review*, beginning in the September issue of 1919, and later as a book in 1936.

The Chinese Written Language as a Medium for Poetry.

This Twentieth Century not only turns a new page in the Book of the World, but opens another and a startling chapter. Vistas of strange futures unfold for man, of world-embracing cultures half-weaned from Europe, of hitherto undreamed responsibilities for nations and races.

Especially for Great Britain and for the United States it sounds a note of hope, and, at the same time, a note of warning. They alone, of modern peoples, still bear aloft the torch of freedom, advance the banner of individual culture. They alone, perhaps, possess the tolerance and the sympathy required to understand the East, and to lift her into honorable sisterhood. The peoples of Continental Europe fear the possibilities of selfhood in the East; therefore they

1.   Fenollosa's draft, "The Chinese Written Language as a Medium for Poetry," p. 1. Reproduced from B101 F4248, Yale Collection of American Literature, Beinecke Rare Book and Manuscript Library.

aim to crush her, before her best powers
shall have time to ripen.

Strange as it may seem, the future of
Anglo-Saxon supremacy in the world is probably
bound up with the future of that East. If the
better elements in her be crushed, and the
worse be chained in slavery to some Western
form of Despotism, time may come to blow
out our torch. Far beyond a sentimental sympathy, our loyalty to our own ideals should
urge us to champion the cause of China's
independence, to nourish and expand the
germs of her own best thought and aim, and
finally to help her merge them into the heritage
of our own freedom.

(This Chinese problem, alone, is so vast that
it dominates the world, and forces on that
supreme historical crisis which has been
waiting for centuries. No nation can afford
to ignore it; we in America least of all. We
must face it across the Pacific, and master it
or it will master us. And the only way to
master it is to strive with patient sympathy
to understand the best, the most hopeful,
and the most human elements in it.)

It is unfortunate that England and
America have ignored or mistaken, so long,

2. Fenollosa's draft, "The Chinese Written Language as a Medium for Poetry," p. 2. Reproduced from B101 F4248, Yale Collection of American Literature, Beinecke Rare Book and Manuscript Library.

This Chinese problem, alone, is so vast that it dominates the world, and forces on that supreme historical crisis which has been waiting for centuries. No nation can afford to ignore it; we in America least of all. We must face it across the Pacific, and master it—or it will master us. And the only way to master it is to strive with patient sympathy to understand the best, the most hopeful, and the most human elements in it.

What caught my eye was the second and third passages, which had been crossed out with a slash of pencil:

Especially for Great Britain and for the United States, it sounds a note of hope, and, at the same time, a note of warning. They alone, of modern people, still bear aloft the torch of freedom, advance the banner of individual culture. They alone, perhaps, possess the tolerance and the sympathy required to understand the East, and to lift her into honorable sisterhood. The peoples of Continental Europe fear the possibilities of selfhood in the East; therefore they aim to crush her, before her best powers shall have time to ripen.

Strange as it may seem, the future of Anglo Saxon supremacy in the world is probably bound up with the future of that East. If the better elements in her be crushed, and the worse be chained in slavery to some Western form of Despotism, time may come to blow out our torch. Far beyond a sentimental sympathy, our loyalty to our own ideals should urge us to champion the cause of China's independence, to nourish and expand the germs of her own best thought and aim, and finally to help her merge them into the heritage of our own freedom.

After studying carefully the other traces of editing among Fenollosa's papers, I came to the conclusion that the pencil mark was characteristically the editor Pound's. But then the question was: What shall I do with these two deleted passages that sound such a grating note of cultural supremacism?

It is certainly important to situate Fenollosa in his own historical moment, which was a time when the doors to the Far East were forced open by cannons and when Marco Polo's fantastic Cathay became a map of many pieces of land that one could either possess as a colonist or traverse as a tourist. What Fenollosa called "a new page in the book of the world" was indeed an epoch characterized by a mixture of colonial violence and centennial vision. It is therefore quite tempting to make a seemingly sound argument for the cultural imperialist implications in Fenollosa's work. But where might such historical recontextualization or ideological thematization lead us? In this *predetermined* interpretative structure, is there any room for a history of texts, texts that are never simply documents of historic events or extralinguistic reality but rather whose own movement is always already history itself?

Here I find myself agreeing with Greenblatt when he calls for a resistance to a priori ideological determinism. In his study of transatlantic migrations, which has remained an important inspiration for my current project, Greenblatt writes: "Representational practices are ideologically significant... but I think it is important to resist what we may call a priori ideological determinism, that is, the notion that particular modes of representation are inherently and necessarily bound to a given culture or class or belief system, and that their effects are unidirectional" (1991, 4).

It is true that Fenollosa's—or, for that matter, twentieth-century America's—ethnographic representation of Asia is inseparable from the various forms of colonialism; the fact that I explore in this book the ethnographic aspect of American literature—an aspect manifesting itself not only in what literary works say but also in what they *do*— bespeaks the significance of cultural framework. But, like Greenblatt, I am not convinced by any study that, however politically sound and logically coherent, reduces literary works to mere cultural symptoms, making representational practices not only semiotically transparent but also ultimately secondary in status to the interpreter's preestablished theoretic frame. Ideological determinism practiced in a simplified political-science fashion makes literary works mere objects of interpretation, rather than allowing the works themselves to be irreducible, irreplaceable interpretations of culture. In our pursuit of ideological implications and historical contextualizations of literature, we should always remember Clifford Geertz's reminder that "there is nothing so coherent as a paranoid's delusion or a swindler's story."[18]

What the two missing paragraphs of Fenollosa's essay and the editorial markings represent, I believe, is a history of transpacific displacement, whose significance lies less in the essay's immediate ideological content than in its mediating, palimpsestical form. The paragraphs epitomize the meandering trajectories of America's transpacific imaginations of the past century and embody in the most concrete terms the tortuousness of the path to cross-cultural understanding. As the early chapters of this book show, what may seem to be merely stylistic, editorial choices involved in the Fenollosa / Pound project encapsulate simultaneously the formal complexity of ethnographic writings and the difficulty with which we may come to terms with their ideological content.

The task I set up for myself in this book is to delineate trajectories of textual migrations that may not be easily reducible to a preconceived positivistic history, a history, in Greenblatt's words, that "knows where it is going" (1991, 2). I focus especially on the ways in which different representational practices clash, mix, or struggle with or against one another. Such movements of textual history are driven, I believe, by a strong desire shared by the fundamental goals of anthropological, poetic, and hermeneutic practices—that is, the desire to know the Other, regardless of the different means by which such acts of knowing take place: whether to describe ethnographically, idealize poetically, or interpret hermeneutically. To appropriate the Other's representational practices, or to learn the Other's ways of imagining the world, proves to be, as most of the authors I study in this book have realized, one of the best routes to getting to the essence of the Other. The three ethnographers to be considered in chap-

18. Clifford Geertz, *The Interpretation of Cultures* (New York: BasicBooks, 1973), 18.

ter 1 (Percival Lowell, Ernest Fenollosa, and Florence Ayscough) believed that the essence of Oriental cultures lies in their identifiable linguistic patterns. These ethnographers, in my reading, laid the groundwork for the ethnographic enterprise of the Imagist poets.

Chapter 2, "Ezra Pound: An Ideographer or Ethnographer?" examines the multiple roles played by the Imagist Pound in such an enterprise. I argue that Pound's Imagism constitutes a modern ethnography that reinvents an "image" of Oriental linguistic culture. His editing of Fenollosa's manuscripts continues the transpacific dislocation and relocation of cultural meanings from Chinese to Japanese to American (Li Po–Mori–Fenollosa–Pound). And his vision of a world civilization, *paideuma* (a concept he inherits from the German Diffusionist anthropologist Leo Frobenius), relies on gleaning textual samples from an immense variety of cultures, samples that Pound hopes can transcend their cultural and historical particularities but that ultimately fail to do so.

Chapter 3, "The Intertextual Travel of Amy Lowell," traces Lowell's footsteps in Oriental linguistic landscapes, including her correspondence with her brother Percival, who lived in and wrote about Japan and Korea, and her collaboration with Florence Ayscough in the translation of Chinese poetry. Without knowing the languages, Lowell's translations and her poetry, such as *Pictures of the Floating World*, which imagines the Far East, rely not only on the work of her "tour guides" (Percival and Ayscough), but also on popular "tourist guidebooks," that is, travel writings and ethnographic accounts.

But twentieth-century American literature's transpacific experience does not end with Imagism. Starting with chapter 4, I make the transition to other textual trajectories. In this chapter, entitled "The Multifarious Faces of the Chinese Language," I first compare two radically different conceptualizations of the Chinese language: those of Imagism and American popular novels and movies, such as the Charlie Chan series. Whereas the latter pidginizes and stigmatizes the racial Other's language, the former incorporates Chinese linguistic features into its own modernist poetic innovation by means of ventriloquism. I then argue that both conceptualizations become a concern in the work of Asian American essayist Lin Yutang and poet John Yau. Lin advocates Pidgin English, a hybrid of Chinese and English, as a more expressive language than standard English. He is critical of the tendency to standardize English by purging the so-called linguistic pollutants—that is, the kind of English spoken by immigrants and foreigners who, in Henry James's words, have played with the English language, "dump[ing] their mountain of promiscuous material into the foundations of the American."[19] Likewise, Yau has also engaged critically with mainstream American views of the Chinese language. By further pidginizing Charlie Chan's pidginization and doubly ventriloquizing Imagism's ventriloquism, Yau's poetry calls into question language's ties to race and ethnicity and makes an even stronger case for what we have already witnessed in Imagism: the fluidity of the migration of cultural meanings.

Chapter 5, "Maxine Hong Kingston and the Making of an 'American' Myth," argues that while Kingston's fiction claims to represent an extralinguistic "Asian American" experience, the textual experience of her work is largely American, and canonically so. The making of an American text is achieved by filling in the fractures between "source materials" and erasing the linguistic foreignness embodied by those materials. When intertextual trajectories are concealed, Kingston's work becomes a transparent representation of the so-called universal human experience championed by mainstream American literature.

Chapter 6, "Translation as Ethnography: Problems in American Translations of Contemporary Chinese Poetry," argues that American translators' thematic approach to contemporary Chinese poetry, which ignores the poetry's formal innovation and its cultural implications, constitutes an ethnographic account of contemporary China. Instead of allowing the "foreign" linguistic and cultural elements to come into the body of the English translation and thus open up the potentialities of

19. Henry James, *The Question of Our Speech* (Boston: Houghton Mifflin, 1905), 43.

the English language, the translators smooth over the difficulties of linguistic and cultural translation by adopting thematic approaches and producing "clean," "uncontaminated" texts. The resulting trajectories of intercultural migration remain concealed and the politics of intertextual displacement unexplored.

The writers I study and the methodology by which my study has been conducted are inevitably bound up with my own life and my own perception of the world. Whether it is the story of my old neighbor or the formation of American literature, my focus remains on the ways that the incessant migration and displacement of cultural meanings have taken place and the ways that such dislocation and relocation have been accounted for. To read these texts as travel narratives in the extraordinary sense is on the one hand to undermine the truth claims made in cultural descriptions based on the simple fact that the writers "have been there" and on the other hand to underscore the power that writing exercises over the construction of reality. It is true that many of the writers whom I study have never been to the Far East, a place that lies at the heart of their imagination and writing, but that is not the point. Somehow they manage to travel, see, know, and tell in ways that may appear different, but not different enough from those of ordinary travelers. Their extraordinary modes of travel in the world of texts, as it were, reflect our own intertextual modes of travel and expose our blindness to our own ways of seeing.

Having lived myself for nearly nine years now in the United States, or Meiguo, which my younger self had wished the old man could describe for me, I often think of him, of his Meiguo and mine. It pains me sometimes to realize how insensitive we are to our ways of conceptualizing the world. By writing this book, which is less about what people see than about how they see, less about the migrations of people than about the migrations of texts—texts do not just document history; their own movement is, I stress, history itself—I want to pay a long-overdue tribute to my old neighbor, whom I discredited out of my own ignorance and who sees, just as we all do, differently.

ONE

Ethnographers-Out-There

Percival Lowell, Ernest Fenollosa, and Florence Ayscough

Under present conditions a more extended knowledge of
East Asiatic cultures seems to be a matter of great national
importance. Our commerce and political intercourse with
Eastern Asia are rapidly expanding, and in order to deal
intelligently with the problems arising in this area we require
a better knowledge of the people and of the countries with
which we are dealing. This is true of China and Japan, and
this is true of our Malay possessions.

Franz Boas, "A Plea for a
Great Oriental School" (1903)

Franz Boas's 1903 vision for a deepened and expanded American understanding of Asia was anticipated, corroborated, and inherited by the
many ethnographers, travelers, scholars, diplomats, and missionaries
who went across the Pacific Ocean around the turn of the century. Some
ethnographers even worked to a great extent in the fashion of Boasian
cultural and linguistic anthropology, whose essential doctrine lies in
identifying cultural traits in linguistic patterns. The ethnographers I
study in this chapter, namely Percival Lowell, Ernest Fenollosa, and Flor-

ence Ayscough, are three who followed Boas's lead. In a quintessential Boasian manner, they chose language as a path to the heart of the culture they wanted to describe. Although it is true that none of them had any institutional affiliations with the Boasian School, the fact scarcely diminishes the significance of the parallelism between their work and Boasian anthropology; on the contrary, it only strengthens part of my thesis: the study of language and writing, whether as a disciplinary requirement or as an amateurish hobby, constitutes a significant part of the study of culture. It will become increasingly clear as I present my argument that just as Boas recognized the value of linguistic phenomena in ethnology, the writers I study also devoted their attention to Oriental languages, which constitute not just a "medium" for their aesthetic pursuit, but more importantly, an object of their ethnographic vision. "To imagine a language," writes Ludwig Wittgenstein, "means to imagine a form of life."[1]

It may be no mere coincidence that these three figures were all of New England origin: Percival Lowell had in him the famous Boston blue blood; Fenollosa was a native of Salem, Massachusetts; and although Ayscough was born in China, her mother was from Boston, where Ayscough was later educated. With its well-known seaports, New England was at the time a center of trade and contact between the East and West. As Van Wyck Brooks writes in his biography of Fenollosa: "The Far East seemed closer to Salem than to any other American town when Ernest Fenollosa was born there in 1853. While the great East India trade had long since vanished, a considerable stream of commerce still flowed on, and even as late as the eighteen-eighties, two hundred and fifty letters a month left the Salem post-office for India, China and Japan."[2]

How New England wedged itself into the history of the East–West encounter may be encapsulated by this small incident: "The tea that was dumped into Boston harbor on the day of that famous party came off a

1. Ludwig Wittgenstein, *Philosophical Investigations*, trans. G. E. M. Anscombe (New York: Macmillan, 1958), 8e.
2. Van Wyck Brooks, *Fenollosa and His Circle* (New York: E. P. Dutton, 1962), 1.

British ship that had just arrived from Amoy, China."³ After commerce, usually behind cannons, had established contact, people of other walks of life swarmed to the world that previously had existed only in the wildest imaginations. Among these people, secular or religious, were those who set out, as Tennyson described the archetypal voyager Ulysses, to "seek knowledge like a sinking star"; or, as Percival Lowell put it, to "discover...the possibility of using it [the Far East] stereoptically" for ourselves; or to master the emerging problems, lest, as Fenollosa warned, they "master us"; or, as Ayscough suggested, to find reality behind appearances.

. . .

> To say that the Japanese are not a savage tribe is of
> course unnecessary; to repeat the remark, anything but
> superfluous, on the principle that what is a matter of
> common notoriety is very apt to prove a matter about
> which uncommonly little is known. At present we go
> halfway in recognition of these people by bestowing
> upon them a demi-diploma of mental development
> called semi-civilization, neglecting, however, to specify
> in what the fractional qualification consists.
>
> Percival Lowell,
> The Soul of the Far East (1888)

Percival Lowell was in the first group of the so-called Yankee Pilgrims who went to Japan amidst the widespread *japonisme* in the later part of the nineteenth century. The "pilgrims" included Edward Morse, Henry Adams, William Sturgis Bigelow, John La Farge, Lafcadio Hearn, and Ernest Fenollosa.⁴ Lowell arrived in Japan in 1883 and

3. Harold R. Isaacs, *Scratches on Our Minds: American Images of China and India* (New York: John Day, 1958), 67.

4. For an overview of U.S. Orientalism in the late nineteenth century, see T.J. Jackson Lears, *No Place of Grace: Antimodernism and the Transformation of American Culture, 1880–1920* (Chicago: University of Chicago Press, 1994). And for a study of this specific group of Yankee Pilgrims, see Beongcheon Yu, *The Great Circle: American Writers and the Orient* (Detroit: Wayne State University Press, 1983).

spent the next ten years there, during which he was appointed foreign secretary and counselor to the Korean special mission to the United States. I discuss Percival's relation to his sister Amy later, in chapter 3, but it is worth mentioning here that it was through her brother's letters, postcards, and exquisite gifts sent from Japan that young Amy first acquired a taste for the Orient.

Percival Lowell was extremely science minded; later in his life he acquired high standing in astronomy with his work on the observation of Mars and his involvement in the discovery of Pluto. A firm believer in evolutionism and an experienced traveler in the Far East, Lowell wrote a series of book-length accounts of Japan and Korea, including *Chosön* (1886), *The Soul of the Far East* (1888), *Noto* (1891), and *Occult Japan* (1894). Among these, *The Soul of the Far East* received the highest acclaim, praised by Lafcadio Hearn as "the only book of the kind in English" (qtd. in Yu, 115). Read from today's perspective, however, this book is also the most racist of the kind. Its expressed view of the Far Eastern languages, in particular, clearly demonstrates a sense of cultural supremacy. Such a bias will provide a valuable point of reference for Imagism, which drew upon but revised the linguistic conceptualizations delineated by earlier ethnographers like Percival Lowell. Therefore, it is worthwhile to note a few passages from it.

The Soul of the Far East starts with a child's dream come true: "The boyish belief that on the other side of our globe all things are of necessity upside down is startlingly brought back to the man when he first sets foot at Yokohama."[5] The proof for the upside-downness, according to Lowell's observation,[6] is found in the strangeness of these people's language: although standing calmly on their *heads* every day, the natives speak backwards, write backwards, and read backwards (2). The backward order of the language "is but the *a b c* of their contrariety, [because]

5. Percival Lowell, *The Soul of the Far East* (New York: The Macmillan Company, 1911), 1.

6. Ironically, Lowell's "objective" observation is often misleading. What he later believed to be canals on Mars, for instance, turned out to be mere optical illusions.

the inversion extends deeper than mere modes of expression, down into the very matter of thought. Ideas of ours which we deemed innate find in them no home, while methods which strike us as preposterously unnatural appear to be their birthright" (2–3).

The "unnaturalness" also goes well with the "childish," "semi-civilized" features Lowell confers on the Japanese people. It seems that the lack of individuality, or what he terms the "impersonality," is the ultimate indication of the underdevelopment of Japanese culture: "Whether their failure to follow the natural course of evolution results in bringing them in at the death just the same or not, these people are now, at any rate, stationary not very far from the point at which we all set out. They are still in that childish state of development before self-consciousness has spoiled the sweet simplicity of nature. An impersonal race [that] seems never to have fully grown up" (25).

The goal for Lowell's ethnography is stated clearly in the book: "Regarding . . . the Far Oriental as a man . . . we discover in his peculiar point of view a new importance—the possibility of using it stereopti-cally. For his mind-photograph of the world can be placed side by side with ours" (4). One of these stereoptical uses can be found exactly in language; Lowell writes with wry humor: "If it should ever fall to my lot to have to settle that exceedingly vexed Eastern question,—not the emancipation of ancient Greece from the bondage of the modern Turk, but the emancipation of the modern college student from the bond of ancient Greek,—I should propose, as a solution of the dilemma, the addition of a course in Japanese to the college list of required studies" (79). The reason for this seemingly absurd suggestion: "I believe that a study of the Japanese language would prove the most valuable of ponies in the academic pursuit of philology. In the matter of literature, indeed, we should not be adding very much to our existing store, but we should gain an insight into the genesis of speech that would put us . . . at the beginnings of human conversation" (ibid.).

To add the Japanese language to the university curriculum will not enrich "our" literature, Lowell suggests, because "they" do not have any literature. But the knowledge of this language that is spoken, written, and read backwards may illustrate the primitive stage of humanity and facilitate the appreciation of "our" own far more advanced tongue.

Lowell was not alone in degrading Oriental languages. Among the Yankee Pilgrims, Edward Morse held a similar view of Chinese. In his voluminous published journal, *Japan Day by Day* (1917), Morse inserted a lengthy footnote about the Chinese language that would have raised the hackles of the later Imagists:

> It should be constantly borne in mind that the characters used by the Japanese are strictly Chinese. So far as I know the Japanese never invented a character any more than we have ever invented a letter; the Japanese did, however, invent an alphabet by using Chinese characters in reference to their sound and finally abbreviated them into a single stroke or two; this the Chinese never did. Even with the example of a phonetic system—the Sanscrit—on their western borders, not one of the hundred millions had the ingenuity to devise an alphabet of their own. Dr. S. Wells Williams, the great sinologist, says their language has shut them from their fellow men more than any other cause, and Colonel Garrick Mallory, an authority on picture writing and hieroglyphics, says the practice of pictography does not belong to civilization. The question arises in regard to the Chinese: Is the nation inert and backward on account of their method of writing or are the people fossilized and cannot adopt another method? A Japanese scholar informed me that the Japanese language was much impeded in its development by the introduction of Chinese characters. (169)

Such a degrading account of the Other by way of its language, commonly found in colonialist texts, was contradicted by writers such as Ernest Fenollosa and Florence Ayscough. Later, the Imagists relied on but revised these precursory texts and discourses. Whether or not the poets inherited more biases than they actually rejected, there is a picture that becomes clear: Imagism emerged from an active dialogue with the earlier ethnographies and with their conflicting views of the

Other's linguistic culture. As I argue, the Imagists were indeed making their own versions of ethnography by intertextually appropriating previous ones.

. . .

> An ideograph does not make upon the Japanese brain any impression similar to that created in the Occidental brain by a letter or combination of letters—dull, inanimate symbols of vocal sounds. To the Japanese brain an ideograph is a vivid picture: it lives; it speaks; it gesticulates.
>
> *Lafcadio Hearn*, Glimpses of Unfamiliar Japan *(1894)*

> Thinking is thinging.
>
> *Ernest Fenollosa, editorial in the* Golden Age *(June 1906)*

Ernest Fenollosa (1853–1908), whose name came down to us in canonical literary history mainly through one monograph promoted by Ezra Pound, was, in his own right, one of the key figures in America's transpacific experience. After graduating from Harvard with first-class honors in philosophy and spending two more years there as a graduate resident in the same field, he turned his attention to art and studied at the Massachusetts Normal Art School. In 1877, Fenollosa was recommended to fill the first chair of philosophy at Tokyo University and thus embarked on his transpacific career.

Steeped in Emersonian Transcendentalism, Fenollosa spent the next two decades searching for the truth that he believed to be embodied universally in Oriental and Occidental art, philosophy, and language. In the field of art, Fenollosa obtained such high esteem in Japan that he was appointed Imperial Commissioner of Fine Arts by the emperor and became an authority who issued certificates of authenticity for Japanese art pieces to the Japanese. Taking advantage of being an American during Japan's craze for Westernization, he tried to redirect the development of Japanese art to the "original"—as opposed to Westernized—expressions.[7] Finding the authentic, native Oriental culture became the lifetime mission of this devout follower of Transcendentalism. It was in the same spirit, "to strive with patient sympathy to understand the best, the most hopeful and the most human elements," that he set out for another venture—the study of Chinese poetry and language.

Fenollosa lived at a time when the contact of the two hemispheres had resulted in either bloody conflicts or blatant shows of force: China and Great Britain fought two opium wars between 1840 and 1860, Commodore Perry's gunships opened Imperial Japan's gate in 1853, and Westerners were killed by Chinese Boxer rebels. Such violence, Fenollosa believed, could have been avoided had the West been able to comprehend the culture of the East. As a result, many of his writings contain a mixed sense of historical urgency and transcendental vision. He was remarkable not only for never losing sight of his goal—the "soul of the Far East," to use P. Lowell's phrase—but also for possessing a clear self-awareness about the method of his pursuit. Facing the vast corpus of Asian culture, Fenollosa chose as his tool of understanding something that had been ignored by his predecessors for centuries—language and literature. There are numerous examples that illustrate unequivocally his awareness of the significance of language and literature to his ambitious ethnographic project. In one of his many unpublished notebooks, eight pages of "Notes for a General Article on Chinese Poetry" dated October 14, 1900, contain the following passages written in Fenollosa's cursive hand (but erased by Pound's strong, blue pencil mark):[8]

> I write, not as a sinologue, who knows the language, and the fine points in the language; but rather as a student of literature and of the relation of literature to national ideals and life....

7. Lawrence Chisolm, *Fenollosa: The Far East and American Culture* (New Haven: Yale University Press, 1963), 57.

8. I examine some of Pound's intriguing editorial decisions regarding Fenollosa's papers in the next chapter.

The study of Chinese poetry is an important part of the study of Chinese culture. Most of the few English and French translations existent, mostly in prose, give only the universal human content, as it can be understood by the Western mind from its own ideals, and knowing almost nothing of the special world of Chinese conscious-ness. The important thing for us in the West to know, is the richness and tenderness of the Oriental soul. . . .

Indeed, is it not the chief value of travel, and of studying history and alien literatures, that it lifts the veil of our own, necessarily nar-row, local and racial consciousness, and reveals to us over and over a broader human horizon? And as we ascend to the vantage of an observatory on the upper level, how intense is our pleasure to watch grow up from the farthest plain the blue shadow and snowy peaks of a great range of human world whose Existence we have hardly suspected! (B101 F4249)

The same idea is expressed in many other notebooks and drafts of arti-cles, including "Chinese Ideals," an unfinished fifteen-page article on the history of Chinese social and philosophical thoughts; "Chinese Intercourse," two books of notes from his studies of the encounters between the West and China from Ancient Greece to the present day and of their influences upon each other; "Chinese Poetry: Professor Mori's Lectures," three volumes of notes of Mori's lectures on Chinese poetry; and "Chinese Poetry: Translations," two volumes of translation and interpretation of Rihaku's (Li Po's) poetry that Fenollosa tran-scribed from Mori's lectures through Ariga's translation.

Especially noticeable, however, is the 145-page "Notes for a History of the Influence of China upon the Western World."[9] Fenollosa drafted this essay as a lecture to be presented before a seminar he later took at Columbia University. In spite of the title, the essay is more about the history of the Western world's knowledge of China than

9. This essay is another version of the aforesaid "Chinese Intercourse," which is now collected in the Beinecke archive (B99 F4215 and F4216). Since the essay has been tran-scribed by a Japanese scholar, Akiko Murakata, and published in Japan, I quote from

about the history of China's influence. In this historical survey, Fenollosa focuses especially on Western knowledge of the Chinese language—he implicitly situates himself in relation to other well-known travelers to China who have left behind ample ethnographic accounts, which may or may not include a report on the language. He reminded the seminar members at Columbia that "the sole notice of Chinese writing in Europe, up to the 16th C[entury]," could be found in William of Rubruquis, a Franciscan sent by Louis IX of France to the Great Khan in 1253, whose account of China's paper money struck many learned readers as absurd but was corroborated by Marco Polo.[10] In the latter case, despite Polo's central position in the history of Chinese exploration, Fenollosa criticized his contemptible "alien indifference" to Chinese civilization on a simple ground—Polo did not know the language: "It is evident that he was always an alien to the Chinese, and cared nothing for their higher culture. All their religions to him are heathenish; he never spoke or read the Chinese language, and does not even mention their written characters or printed books" (Murakata 73). Whether or not such criticism was based on solid historical evidence—that is, whether or not Marco Polo could, in fact, speak Chinese—is not a crucial matter for this study; instead, what is significant is the fact that Fenollosa passed judgment on a famous traveler on the grounds of the latter's linguistic competence. Fenollosa's historical survey of his predecessors continues along the same line: Mandeville "tells us nothing of the Chinese Literature, language, or mind" (78); the Jesuits started "the transplanting of a knowledge of Chinese language and literature to European scholars" (81); the work of Y. G. Mendoza "has a short but obscure acct. [account] of Chinese characters, in which

Murakata's transcription, which is based on the manuscript in the E. G. Stillman collection at the Houghton Library, Harvard University. Akiko Murakata, ed., *Ernest F. Fenollosa's "Notes for a History of the Influence of China upon the Western World": A Link between the Houghton and the Beinecke Library Manuscripts* (Kyoto, Japan: Kyoto University, 1982).

10. Ibid., 69–70.

it is declared that each word has its peculiar character" (86); and Matthew [i.e., Matteo] Ricci, an Italian Jesuit, "was probably the first to meet and understand the Chinese mind, man to man" (because he not only spoke Chinese fluently but had written fifteen books in the language as well) (94–97). Fenollosa also mentions Bacon, Leibniz, and Voltaire, who were all fascinated by Chinese characters.

It is obvious, then, that Fenollosa launched his venture in Chinese language and poetry because he believed that they contained the essential, "the best, the most hopeful and the most human elements" of Chinese culture. As evident in the following quotation from his "Notes for a General Article on Chinese poetry," he fully realized that "the study of Chinese poetry is an important part of the study of Chinese culture," and he saw himself as "a student of literature and of the relation of literature to national ideals and life." What is crucial, however, is exactly what he had learned or found in Chinese language and poetry. Fenollosa's encounter with Chinese was greatly complicated by the fact that he was learning from a Japanese professor through the mediation of a Japanese translator. A true believer of Platonism would have decried the new version of "three removals" from the truth. But I want to make use of this instance of "removal" to elucidate the complicated process of textual migration set in motion by the desire to describe, to understand, and to appropriate the Other.

Fenollosa started his tutorials first with Mr. Hirai in 1896, and then with Professor Mori in 1899. But he took more serious, systematic lessons with the latter in 1901, right before he left Japan permanently, and it was the 1901 notes that Pound later typed out and unsuccessfully tried to publish. What was relayed to the avid cosmopolitan American student by the Japanese professor on the subject of Chinese poetry is of great significance to the issue at stake.

The three volumes of 1901 notebooks (which, with their water-stained pages, are now in the extensive Pound collection at the Beinecke Library), began with an entry of May 28, the title being written in Fenollosa's cursive hand in pencil: "Professor Mori's Lectures on the History of Chinese Poetry." This first lecture was on the history of the invention and perfection of Chinese characters. A few years later, Fenollosa wrote in *The Chinese Written Character as a Medium for Poetry* (hereafter, *CWC*): "My subject is poetry, not language, yet the roots of poetry are in language. In the study of a language so alien in form to ours as is Chinese in its written character, it is necessary to inquire how these universal elements of form which constitute poetics can derive appropriate nutriment" (10). Such an inquiry into the universal elements of the Chinese language, "the roots of poetry," covered not only a standard introduction to the six methods of inventing Chinese characters, namely *shi ji* (pointing), *sho kei* (referent), *kei sei* (form noise), *kwai i* (meet idea), *jen chu* (convert), *ka sha* (temporary borrow).[11] The tutorial session also emphasized a detail not too conspicuous in the canonical accounts of the history of the language. It is a legend in Pound's transcription:

> The written character is said to have been invented by Soketsu in the time of Kotei, before whose time there had been imperfect expression with signs, or by knots in sting [*sic*], from the days of Fukki and Shinno[.] Soketsu a great genius n subsequent developments made possible by him. Kotei a gt/emperor, not Chinese in origin but believed to have come from West, Sotei [Soketsu] his asst and sec/ possibly of Western origin.
>
> Characters necessitated by having to combine chinese lang/ with "advanced Western thought." Effort to express the thought of one race thru what is comprehensible to another. (B99 F4222)

11. Judging from this entry and several others in Fenollosa's papers, it is certain that both Fenollosa and Pound were aware of the fact that Chinese characters are not completely "pictorial" but at least partly phonetic. This interesting willful "misreading" seems quite common among Western poets, scholars, and philosophers (including Jacques Derrida) who are eager to find an alternative to what Derrida has called logocentricism of alphabet. For more detailed discussion of this issue, see Longxi Zhang, *The Tao and the Logos: Literary Hermeneutics, East and West* (Durham: Duke University Press, 1992). However, as I argue in the next chapter, the overemphasis on the visuality of Chinese characters on the part of Fenollosa and Pound also has to do with the mediation by the Japanese method of reading Chinese texts, a method called *wakun*.

The Japanese tutor seemed to relish the tale that the inventor of Chinese characters was not Chinese in origin and that the written language was created, to quote from another version of Pound's transcription, "to combine the Chinese speech with advanced thought brought in by the western tribe . . . to express the thought of one race through what was comprehensible to another" (ibid.). Fenollosa would later come to realize that "what they then called Western Barbarians may have dwelt inside today's borders of China" (B99 F4223). But the story had a profound attraction for the avid American pupil, because it was, after all, a powerful legend, almost as powerful as the characters themselves, as described in another ancient tale that Fenollosa also noted: "Soketsu's skill in finding the true chord of nature was such that the heavens poured down grain, and the demons of night whine at it. The legend is as old as the characters and scholars take it that the characters have a very deep essence in them, reaching to the essence of the universe and able to bring prosperity, or adversely, misfortune" (B99 F4223).[12]

However, this fantastic legend struck, not the "chord of nature" but rather the chord of culture. Leafing through page after page of Fenollosa's penciled notes, one cannot fail to realize that this Odyssey in Chinese poetry was a quest for what he called the "deep essence" of Chinese humanity, a quest taking place by route of Japanese interpretations. This was not as strange a route to take as it might seem, because the Japanese interpretations of Chinese culture were accorded by the West the highest prestige at the time, as Fenollosa writes,

> One modest merit I may, perhaps, claim for my work: it represents for the first time a Japanese school of study in Chinese cul-

---

12. In another version of Pound's transcription, the passage reads: "Old saying that in inventing the characters SOKETSU struck the chord of the elements so skillfully that heaven cause[d] rain to fall and grain to sprout and the night demons to whine. Meaning the characters reach into spirit of universe, that by them one can cause prosperity or fall into gt/ misfortune" (B99 F4222).

ture. Hitherto Europeans have been somewhat at the mercy of contemporary Chinese scholarship. Several centuries ago China lost much of her creative self, and of her insight into the causes of her own life; but her original spirit still lives, grows, interprets, transferred to Japan in all its original freshness. The Japanese today represent a stage of culture roughly corresponding to that of China under the Sung Dynasty. I have been fortunate in studying for many years as a private pupil under Professor Kainan Mori, who is probably the greatest living authority on Chinese poetry. (*CWC* 10)

And,

> The Chinese themselves have lost the lyrical idealism of their early ages; and we could hardly recover it were it not for its fortunate preservation in Japan. ("Thoughts on Chinese Poetry: Matter for Essays" B100 F4227)

And,

> I wish to illustrate by Japanese examples what must be regarded in their continental range as essentially Chinese ideals; and frequently . . . these ideals can be studied so much more adequately in Japan today than in China, that I have adopted the softer Japanese spelling of Chinese names, a pronunciation indeed much nearer than "Mandarin" to the ancient Chinese sound. ("Chinese Ideals" B98 F4214)

It is hardly my purpose to dismiss the authority of Japanese scholarship; nor is it my intention to present an "original" Chinese interpretation to invalidate the Japanese one. Instead, I am trying to reconstruct part of the transpacific intellectual history, suggesting that the Japanese discourse on the *foreignness* of Chinese culture, a notion that had caught Fenollosa's (and later Pound's) attention, should be understood not only as an expression of Japanese nationalism, but also as an important step in the transpacific displacement of cultural meanings.[13]

In the course of thousands of years of vicissitude caused by emigration, wars, conquests, trades, racial integration, and cultural exchange, the concept of Chineseness has been constantly redefined and China's cultural boundary has never been stable. Native Chinese scholars have seldom been willing to accord enough credence to any notion that might undermine the homogeneity of "Chinese" culture. Yet throughout history, at least in the case of language, there have been numerous moments when Chinese, to borrow Antoine Berman's phrase again, "experiences the foreign." For instance, it is a well-known but never readily acknowledged fact that the encounter with Sanskrit (an alphabetical language), by way of translations from Buddhist texts, made the Chinese linguists after the Han Dynasty realize for the first time that a Chinese character may be pronounced by a combination of vowel and consonant. According to Guangqian Zhu, one of China's best literary theorists and historians of the twentieth century, "without the inspiration from an alphabetic system of writing, it was impossible for Chinese scholars to discover phonetic rules in previously nonphoneticized Chinese characters."[14]

13. For an overview of the Japanese effort to decenter "Chineseness" in order to promote Japanese nationalistic interests by advocating a *toyoshi* (Eastern Asian history), see Stefan Tanaka, *Japan's Orient: Rendering Pasts into History* (Berkeley and Los Angeles: University of California Press, 1993). For a discussion of how modern Japanese historiography proved to be destabilizing to Chinese discourses on the homogeneity of "Chineseness," see D. R. Howland, *Borders of Chinese Civilization: Geography and History at Empire's End* (Durham: Duke University Press, 1996).

14. Guangqian Zhu, *Shilun* (On poetry) (Beijing: Sanlian Shudian, 1985), 220; my translation. See also Lydia Liu, *Translingual Practice: Literature, National Culture, and Translated Modernity—China, 1900–1937* (Stanford: Stanford University Press, 1995). Liu analyzes the historical interactions among China, Japan, and the West in terms of translingual practice, a process by which new words, meanings, discourses, and modes of representation arose, circulated, and acquired legitimacy in early modern China as it contacted/collided with European/Japanese languages and literatures (26).

In contrast to China-centered native intellectuals, Japanese scholars, whose own culture has been profoundly influenced by the Chinese, have been more ready to propagate the discourse on the heterogeneity of "Chineseness." In Fenollosa's notes, for instance, is an entry dated around September 7, 1901: "During Sei and Rio, great thing was made in Buddhism, & with Sanskrit language—& Shugio was a great scholar in Sanskrit characters—he applied the pronunciation of the Sanskrit language to the pronunciation of the characters of China" (B100 F4226).

Indeed, throughout Japanese history, scholars of nationalistic persuasion often asserted that Chinese written characters were of a nonnative origin. Ogyu Sorai of the eighteenth century, for instance, believed that Chinese characters had originated from an explicitly foreign environment.[15] In the late nineteenth and early twentieth centuries, especially, when Japanese nationalism was on the steady rise, the historian Shiratori Kurakichi (1865–1942), among others, tried to decenter Chineseness by arguing that some key historical figures of ancient China, such as Yao, Shun, and Yu (the three ancient emperors), were anthropomorphic manifestations of ancient ideals that could be traced to those of the Aryan and Semitic, that is "Western," races. Shiratori further asserted that "before true metaphysical concepts were introduced, China's intellectual world was limited to a form of shamanism similar to the heaven worship of the Northern barbarians" (Tanaka 117–21). This statement is congruent with Pound's transcription, "Characters necessitated by having to combine chinese lang/ with 'advanced Western thought.' Effort to express the thought of one race thru what is comprehensible to another." It is then obvious that Fenollosa, studying with Japanese scholars at the time when Japanese nationalism was ascending, picked up the discourse on the foreignness of Chinese language and culture, discourse that would filter through the multilayers of transpacific inter-

15. Naoki Sakai, *Voices of the Past: The Status of Language in Eighteenth-Century Japanese Discourse* (Ithaca: Cornell University Press, 1991), 218.

textual metamorphosis and contribute to the creation of some peculiar ethnographic images of China in twentieth-century America.

If I were teaching Chinese students about the intimate relationship between the English language and American individualistic culture, I might use this example: The English word *INDIVIDUALISM* contains four I's (first-person singular pronoun). In this case, would I be accused of misrepresentation since the capitalization of every *i* in *individualism* occurs only rarely in English? Or would I be acquitted of blame because my need to illuminate cultural interpretations should justify my sleight of hand, especially since, after all, INDIVIDUALISM can be so written? They are questions to keep in mind when we examine Fenollosa's article on the Chinese written character, which has now become a literary monument through Pound's editing hand.

Part of the thesis Fenollosa advanced in this article is the closeness of the Chinese language to nature as evidenced by the formation of sentences as well as by the construction of individual characters. He starts out with a general statement on the sentence form (*CWC* 16):

> The sentence form was forced upon primitive men by nature itself. It was not we who made it; it was a reflection of the temporal order in causation. All truth has to be expressed in sentences because all truth is the *transference of power.* The type of sentence in nature is a flash of lightning. It passes between two terms, a cloud and the earth. No unit of natural process can be less than this.... Their unit of process can be represented as:

term	*transference*	*term*
from	*of*	*to*
which	*force*	*which*

If we regard this transference as the conscious or unconscious act of an agent we can translate the diagram into:

agent	*act*	*object*

While such transference of power is a universal determinative of sentence structure, Chinese, Fenollosa claims, has the advantage over English of being able to construct a sentence visually, such as 日上東 (see fig. 3).[16] But this is barely a Chinese sentence; it is not an idiomatic expression. Fenollosa should have known that "Sun rises in the east" could be expressed in Chinese as in the following lines, which he had learned from his Japanese masters and had copied down in his notebooks (see fig. 4):

nichi	*shutsu*	*to*	*nan*	*gu*
sun	rises	East	south	corner

The sun rises in the south east corner.[17]

Or,

Nichi	*shutsu*	*to*	*ho*	*nai*
sun	go out	east	direction	corner

The sun rises out of an eastern corner (angle).[18]

But 出 (*shutsu;* go out) does not work so well as 上 (rise) to fit into a well-wrought analysis like this:

> "The Sun rises in the East." Here Sun, which already means "shining" enters in the most picturesque way into the character for East, shining entangled in the branches of a tree. There is something dazzling in the repetition, something like the concentrated rays that come from diamonds. Moreover there is homology between the upright line of the rising, and the upright growing line of the tree. If we should add an horizon line across the roots of the tree, the sun would just take the place of the dot in the second character. (B99 F4219)

---

16. I am quoting from Fenollosa's manuscript version of the article, which has a Chinese character different from the one used in Pound's version. More on this interesting variation appears in chapter 2.

17. B100 F4232, "Okagura, Sogioku and Others, Notebook."

18. B100 F4235, "Mori and Ariga Notebook," vol. 1.

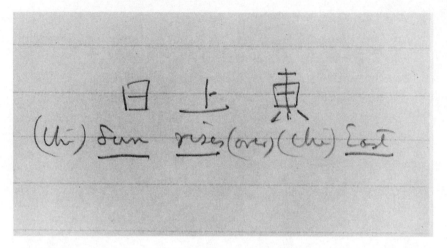

3.   Fenollosa, "(The) Sun rises (over) (the) East." Reproduced from B99 F4218, vol. 2, facing p. 50, Yale Collection of American Literature, Beinecke Rare Book and Manuscript Library.

Allow me to speculate how this perfect homology might be created. As we see in figure 4, Fenollosa was studying a poem entitled 陌上桑 (Ballad of the Mulberry Road). If we replace the 出 in the first line with the 上 in the title and cut off the other two characters, we can easily have 日上東. Indeed, 上, with its sunlike dot above the horizon, works better than 出, because the latter visually does not conform to the "homology" and etymologically is related to growing plants, rather than to dazzling sunshine.[19] Or, another line of speculation is possible: if, for instance, you write the English sentence "Sun rises in the East" on a slip of paper and hand it over to someone who knows some Chinese and some English, someone like Mr. Ariga, the mediator, isn't it possible that you may end up getting a "crib" such as

19.   If this instance of fabrication is troubling, then the other in the same essay may be more so. According to Achilles Fang, the beautiful poem used in Fenollosa's essay as a supreme model for Chinese classics, namely, the poem beginning with "Moon rays like pure snow," was actually written by an eleven-year-old Japanese boy (Achilles Fang, "Fenollosa and Pound," *Harvard Journal of Asiatic Studies* 20 [1957]: 217).

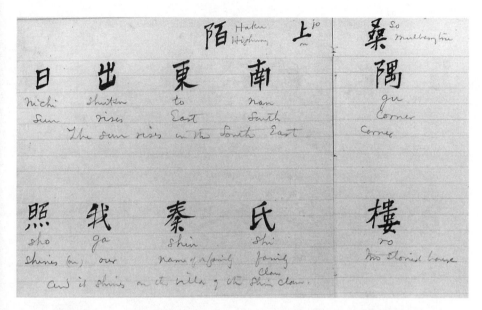

4.   A page from Fenollosa's "Okakura, Sogioku and Others, Notebook." Reproduced from B100 F4232, Yale Collection of American Literature, Beinecke Rare Book and Manuscript Library.

日上東? An anthropologist may give a hearty laugh here, because misleading a native informant intentionally or unintentionally with questions steeped in the anthropologist's preconceptions is by no means an uncommon practice in fieldwork. Or, interpreters may insert themselves in the middle of cross-cultural interactions and even invent something as they go along. Boas has forewarned in his introduction to the *Handbook of American Indian Languages*:

> Another difficulty which often develops whenever the investigator works with a particularly intelligent interpreter is, that the interpreter imbibes too readily the views of the investigator, and that his information, for this reason, is strongly biased, because he is not so well able to withstand the influence of formative theories as the trained investigator ought to be. Anyone who has carried on work with intelligent Indians will recall instances of this kind, where the inter-

preter may have formulated a theory based on the questions that
have been put through him, and has interpreted his answers under
the guidance of his preconceived notions. (59–60)

It is hard to figure out whether it was the investigator or the interpreter who had fabricated the "Chinese" material here. There are no
tape recordings of the tutorial sessions; only Fenollosa's notes give some
clue as to what was going on in his mind when he asked those questions.
The following is a list of "Questions to Ask Mr. Ariga," which Fenollosa
jotted down in his notebook:

Chinese characters—no difference of nouns or verbs—
Are some words now chiefly nouns, and some chiefly verbs?
In earlier days were nouns derived from verbs?
Order of syntax, almost like English?
Are prepositions verbs? Adjectives.
How is the verb *is* used?
What does the word *not* negative [*sic*].
Is the object generally direct object of the verb?
Can we consider the subject to be thought of as agent?
Sentences often have no subject like Japanese.
In Japanese sentence, is subject often nonexistent?
Is there the thought of the active verb, a passive one?
Is *Onnism* a copula? Does it denote existence?
Aninno[?] a new honoric form
Is the verbal idea a *becoming*, or an *acting*?
Why does the verb come last? (B100 F4229)

Obviously these are not questions that an ordinary student of language
would ask. The curious questioner has already preconceived some profound philosophical ideas that are waiting to be reincarnated in the
grammar of the foreign language. For indeed these questions are pre-
ceded immediately by another list (ibid.):

THOUGHTS OF WHAT WE OUGHT TO DO

Our aim is to get at ideals of civilization, particularly ideals of man, nature, literature, art.

1. Chinese philosophy...
2. Sketch of Chinese Literature (Belles Lettres)...
3. Study of Chinese Customs ...
4. Study of Chinese History

What this list reveals is undoubtedly the larger, ethnographic framework for the seemingly simple linguistic puzzles. If we recall some of the assertions made in *CWC*, which was written around 1901, it is obvious that seeds of those assertions had already been planted in the list of language questions designed sometime in 1898, when Fenollosa knew hardly any Chinese.[20] The 1898 questions suggest (or anticipate?) the possibility that Chinese characters, including verbs, nouns, prepositions, and adjectives, may be verbal in nature; in the 1901 article, the verbalness of Chinese becomes a major argument. The question was put before he knew the language: "How is the verb *is* used?" and here is the assertion made in the article:

> In Chinese the chief verb for "is" not only means actively "to have," but shows by its derivation that it expresses something even more concrete, namely "to snatch from the moon with the hand." 有 Here the baldest symbol of prosaic analysis is transformed by magic into a splendid flash of concrete poetry. (*CWC* 19)

To the question "What does the word *not* negative [negate]?" we have this answer two years later:

> In nature there are no negations, no possible transfers of negative force. The presence of negative sentences in language would seem to corroborate the logicians' view that assertion is an arbitrary subjec-

---

20. The list of "Questions to Ask Mr. Ariga" is not dated in the notebook entitled "Notes and Translations" (B100 F4229), but the page containing the list is located between notes dated April 6, 1898, and those dated May 9, 1898.

tive act. *We* can assert a negation, though nature can not. But here again science comes to our aid against the logician: all apparently negative or disruptive movements bring into play other positive forces. It requires great effort to annihilate. Therefore we should suspect that, if we could follow back the history of all negative particles, we should find that they also are sprung from transitive verbs. It is too late to demonstrate such derivations in the Aryan languages, the clue has been lost; but in Chinese we can still watch positive verbal conceptions passing over into so-called negatives. Thus in Chinese the sign meaning "to be lost in the forest" relates to a state of non-existence. (*CWC* 18–19)

It seems that Fenollosa was expecting Ariga's answers to substantiate his broad thesis on the universality of world civilization, a thesis derived from Emersonian Transcendentalism. Fenollosa found the universality in language in what he called the "universal grammar." In a notebook that contains one version of *CWC*, on facing pages, Fenollosa wrote 日上東 on the verso and the following passage on the recto as an explanation of this "exemplary" Chinese sentence:[21]

But now if single Chinese words have such synthetic power, this power becomes highly increased when we put words together into a sentence form. Here in its syntax still now light is thrown by Chinese upon universal grammar.

We open here an interesting inquiry, with which grammarians seldom trouble themselves, why the sentence form should exist *at all*, why all languages should have it, and what is the normal type of it. If it is so universal, it ought to correspond to some primary fact in nature. (B99 F4218)

It was probably this inquiry into the "universal grammar" that had led Fenollosa to identify willfully three "suns" in a single Chinese

21. It was Fenollosa's habit to write mainly on the right-hand pages, leaving the left-hand pages for annotations and illustrations.

sentence and then use the sentence to illustrate the natural transference of power as in the diagram: agent——>act——>object (*CWC* 16). Adding a preposition could have made the sentence sound more idiomatic in Chinese, such as 日上於東, but the magical effect would have been lost and the natural transference of power would have been interrupted.

Yet, it is pointless to accuse Fenollosa of committing forgery if we understand the word "forgery" only in the pejorative sense of "fabrication" but not in the positive sense of "invention." It is almost impossible to set the record straight because there is no record that is not caught in an endless intertextual cross-reference. From the Chinese legends to the Japanese interpretation, to Fenollosa's reinterpretation of his Japanese masters' and translators' words, to his re-creation of what are Chinese character and poetry, and later to Pound's tinkering with Fenollosa's manuscripts, what has taken place, and continues to take place, are not simple acts of forgery, but a complicated process of producing cultural descriptions along the meandering trajectories of textual migration.

After all, as the disgruntled Pound wrote circa 1958 in response to Achilles Fang's criticism of Fenollosa: "The latest opponent to Fenollosa's perceptions seems to have overlooked the title of the essay: which states that the ideogram is considered 'as a medium for poetry.' . . . He never claimed that cheap journalists or pedants made use of the resource mentioned" (B103 F4275).

As a medium for poetry, the Chinese language could "bear" 日上東 as a sentence although it hardly is one. It is like, for the sake of better illustration in ethnography, writing INDIVIDUALISM so that it becomes an embodiment of four I's and of the essence of an individualistic culture. To dismiss 日上東 as a non-Chinese sentence is only to assert that there is a difference between this sentence and, say, 日上於東, which is more idiomatically Chinese. But who is to decide Chineseness when even the Chinese characters were supposedly invented by "Soketsu in the time of Kotei," both of whom "came from the West"? According to some records, the so-called Western Barbarians "may have dwelt inside today's borders of China," so it is the border that has been shifting. Does it make the inventor of characters "Chinese" or not? Endless cross-reference of this kind reveals the shifting grounds on which any essentialized ethnographic claim will have to stand at its own peril, grounds that move as constantly as the boundaries of nation, language, or text.

. . .

> Men of different races have essayed, are essaying, the
> ascent of this mountain [of Perfected Civilization]; many
> paths have been mapped along its rugged sides; and
> although none ignore the irregularity of natural terrain,
> the paths, we hope, show an upward tendency. They dif-
> fer greatly in character but lead towards a common goal;
> and if the summit of this fair mountain is to be attained,
> is it not essential that travellers upon these varied paths
> report not only the nature of the progress they have
> each accomplished, but also advise as to the vehicles they
> have found an effective means of progression?
> *Florence Ayscough, "Proem," in* Within the
> Walls of Nanking *(1928)*

Both being crucial transpacific go-betweens, Florence Ayscough and Ernest Fenollosa have enjoyed strikingly different literary fates. Whereas the names of Fenollosa and Pound are now like a Chinese-character scroll distich hanging in the hall of fame of American literature—and Fenollosa will always be remembered as long as Pound is— Ayscough has been consigned to oblivion, to the other side of Lethe along with her collaborator, Amy Lowell. But, for a time, both Ayscough and Lowell were energetic and aspiring travelers on the transpacific routes. Apart from their individual work, their collaboration on the Chinese translation has created a modern poetics and ethnography just as important as the Pound / Fenollosa project, which has always been adulated as a superior comparison by the biased (mostly gender-biased) critics. I shall discuss their collaboration in chapter 3, where I study Lowell, and focus here on Ayscough's own writings about China.

Florence Wheelock (1875–1942) was born in Shanghai, China, to a Canadian father from New Brunswick and an American mother from New England.[22] She finished her college education in Boston, where she became a friend of Amy Lowell. At the age of twenty-three, she returned to Shanghai with her newly wed English husband, Francis Ayscough. During the next four decades, Florence Ayscough grew increasingly famous as a Sinologist and translator with her prodigious publications: she published many books and translations of both scholarly and popular nature on various Chinese subjects, among which are *Fir-Flower Tablets* (1921), *A Chinese Mirror: Being Reflections of the Reality behind Appearance* (1925), *Tu Fu* (1929), and *Chinese Women: Yesterday and Today* (1937). She also became an honorable member of the Royal Asiatic Society, giving lectures all over the world (Shanghai, New York, Chicago, Boston, London, Vienna, Berlin, and Vancouver, among other places). But what especially draws my attention is her method of representation. It is her particular way of describing the intimate details of China that brings her work closer to Imagism's poetic ethnography.

It is true that much of Ayscough's work falls somewhere between scholarly ethnographic accounts and popular travel writings, and that her career blossomed during a time when American tourism to the Far East was on the rise.[23] Nevertheless, by insisting on its own mode of representation, by foregrounding a feature I discuss presently, Ayscough's writing about China manages at times to distinguish itself from both an Old China Hand's groping amongst antique bones and a populist's catering to the thirst for exoticism. In *A Chinese Mirror*, in particular, she embarks upon a large-scale ethnographic project, intending to catch glimpses into the Chinese realities.

---

22. Florence Wheelock Ayscough MacNair was her full name at the time of death.
23. More on the possible historical recontextualization appears in chapter 3.

"A mirror in China is no mere sheet of glass, backed with mercury and designed to reflect the perfect features of a lovely woman." Thus opens the 464-page book. "It is used, among its varied functions, for such a purpose, but generally speaking, a mirror has more serious work to do."[24] And an example of such serious work is that a "Chinese mirror" enables her, as an ethnographer, to see what may be invisible to others: "China is usually treated by the West from a purely academic point of view; that is, her art, literature and archaeology are studied as are similar objects connected with dead civilizations; but China is alive, and she is virile; moreover, her ancient beliefs and thoughts are indissolubly knit into the life of her people. Therefore I have tried to make the country, as I know it, seem a living entity to my readers" (15–16).

But what exactly is the nature of this magic mirror she holds in her hand that can make China appear alive on pages? She explains:

> One of the means by which I have striven to attain this end is
> through strict observance of idiom in translation; believing, as I do,
> that the genius of a language appears in its idiom, I have done my
> utmost to preserve that of the Chinese. The translations with the
> few exceptions specifically noted are my own, and I have found that
> in many cases I can approximate far more closely to the Chinese
> idiom if, instead of rendering an ideograph by any one English
> word, although it be universally accepted as an equivalent, I use a
> phrase based on the analysis of the ideograph, or "character" as it is
> generally called. (16)

" 'Character' as it is generally called" alludes, no doubt, to Fenollosa's influential essay, a parallel project with which hers would ineluctably be compared. As it turns out, Ayscough is just as straightforward as her fellow traveler in expounding the linguistic approach to ethnography. In Fenollosa's case, it is called the ideogrammic method; in hers, ideo-

---

24. Florence Ayscough, *A Chinese Mirror: Being Reflections of the Reality behind Appearances* (Boston: Houghton Mifflin, 1925), 9.

graphic analysis. To explain further this method, she quotes a long passage from her own introduction to *Fir-Flower Tablets*, a book of Chinese poems translated into English:

> It must not be forgotten that Chinese is an ideographic, or picture language. These marvellous collections of brush-strokes which we call Chinese characters are really separate pictographic representations of complete thoughts. Complex characters are not spontaneously composed, but are built up of simple characters, each having its own peculiar meaning and usage; these, when used in combination, each play their part in modifying either the sense or sound of the complex. Now it must not be thought that these separate entities make an overloud noise in the harmony of the whole character. They are each subdued to the total result, the final meaning, but they do produce a qualifying effect upon the word itself. Since Chinese characters are complete ideas, it is convenient to be able to express the various degrees of these ideas by special characters which shall have these exact meanings; it is therefore clear that to grasp a poet's full intention in a poem there must be a knowledge of the analysis of characters.[25]

This seeming digression from the focus of ethnography by bringing in terms used in literary translation is not at all a confusion on Ayscough's part; instead, the method of ideographic analysis provides her reliable access to the Chinese reality she is trying to grasp. Examples are numerous:

> China is a land of counter-balance. Its people think in terms of compensation, and its philosophy is founded on a belief in the efficacious interaction of two essences which are called Yang and Yin.... A perfect whole in the Chinese idea consists of the complete fusion of these two essences, each supplied in due proportion, so that the balance is true. *The idiomatic speech of everyday life is full of expressions*

---

25. Quoted in Ayscough, *A Chinese Mirror*, 16–17.

which betray this love of counterpoise. An inquiry is made about size, and
the inquirer asks how "large small" a thing may be—if length is in
question the "long short" is referred to, and the weight is described
as "heavy light." (10; emphasis added)

Or, when she tries to explicate the pyramidal structure of Chinese society, she resorts to the same method:

The four classes of Society who formed the four triangles of the
Chinese Pyramid and whose existence was regarded as vital to the
well-being of the State were:

Scholars (*Shih*). The ideograph is a combination of one and ten,
and suggests, to the Chinese mind, the beginning and end of knowledge.

Farmers (*Nung*). Expressed by the pictogram showing a man
working with his hands at break of day, as the farmer works to this
present.

Labourers (*Kung*). Another pictogram showing a square rule.

Traders (*Shang*). A rather complicated ideograph composed of
"inner" and "words." ("Proem" 14–15)

Such an ethnographic account through linguistic analysis is reminiscent
of P. Lowell's *The Soul of the Far East.* Yet, despite his pretense to linguistic analysis, Lowell reduces his ethnography to a physiological study
of culture, as evident in what he said about the "backward" feature of the
Japanese language and the people alike. By contrast, Ayscough avoids
physiological descriptions of the Chinese and focuses on cultural traits
identifiable in linguistic patterns. In this respect, Ayscough's work parallels what I have described as the core practices of Boasian cultural and
linguistic anthropology, whereas Lowell's inherits nineteenth-century
evolutionist biases.

Clearly, what Ayscough holds in her hand is a *linguistic* "Chinese
mirror," one that reflects "the reality behind any image projected upon
its surface" (*A Chinese Mirror* 9), enabling her to "show certain realities

of Chinese life as they have been manifested to [her]" (10). The symbolic doubling of the deep reality and the surface image is extended to almost all meaningful signs that she encounters. Time and again, she attacks other ethnographers for their ignorance of the symbolism embedded in Chinese life; time and again she strives to understand and explicate the symbols in front of her: "Symbolism of the Purple Forbidden City" (257–340); "the gorgeous colouring of the building is symbolical" (299); "symbols stand on either side of the entrance" (301), and so on. But what's especially interesting is the way in which she unravels these symbols. She often does not task herself directly to explain the symbolism under question; instead, she either uses her Chinese tutor, Mr. Nung Chu (Mr. Cultivator-of-Bamboos), as her mouthpiece or simply paraphrases or quotes directly from Chinese books. Such a feature in her writing might be understood as an expression of desire for authenticity, since quotations or paraphrases are often used by ethnographers to demonstrate the "native view." But it can also be considered an intertextual move by means of which various layers of native discourses become interconnected with the ethnographer's: On the one hand, the symbolism under question is unraveled by a native interpretation; on the other hand, both the unraveled symbolism and its native interpretation become a symbolism on another level—they are cast into a Chinese mirror, through which the ethnographic object is fully illustrated, unraveled.

A quick scan of the overall structure of *A Chinese Mirror* reveals that the book is indeed built on intertextual ground. Six of its seven chapters are in fact travelogues: "The Grass Hut by the Yellow Reach," "The Literary Background of the Great River," "The Chinese Idea of a Garden," "Symbolism of the Purple Forbidden City," "T'ai Shan: The Great Mountain," and "Cult of the Spiritual Magistrates of City Walls and City Moats." As Ayscough makes very clear in her introduction, "While I hope that students of Chinese life and language may find matter of interest in *A Chinese Mirror*, I have tried to make the book untechnical, and have kept the Western traveller very much in mind; for his benefit, too, the maps and diagrams have been included somewhat liberally" (21).

But these are also travelogues modeled on the Chinese tradition of literary tourism. In works of this kind, the traveling narrator follows the footsteps of his predecessors and creates his own travelogue that refers to, comments on, paraphrases, cites, or critiques previous texts.[26] The writing is thus caught up in endless cross-referencing, from which emerges not a single, self-sufficient text, but a chain of intertexts stepping on each other.[27] Similarly, in *A Chinese Mirror*, Ayscough's account of her own tour in China is accompanied frequently by allusions to and quotations from Chinese literature and precursory travel writings by both Chinese and Westerners. For example, on her tour along the Yangtze River, she wrote, "The stretch of country between Tung T'ing Lake and Furze Gate...may seem monotonous, but as Li T'ai-po [Li Po] says, 'From old days until now, people who can really see with their eyes are few,' and in reality it is one of the most interesting parts of the whole stream. Here the world is in the making" (165). And on the same trip, she recorded,

> We steamed away from Fertile Pool in the middle of the afternoon when the sun's rays were just beginning to assume that wonderful slant which glorifies the most unpleasant scene. In the autumn the wild-fowl on this stretch of the river are in myriads. Henry Ellis, who accompanied the embassy under Lord Amherst, dispatched in 1816 by George III to the Emperor of China, writes, "just after sunset the sky was really darkened with flights of wild geese stretching across the horizon." I have often observed the same phenomenon, but strange as it may seem in the case of migratory birds, the flocks have been much smaller since the advent of those colossal cold stor-

26. For discussions and examples of this Chinese genre of travel writing, see Richard E. Strassberg, *Inscribed Landscapes: Travel Writing from Imperial China* (Berkeley and Los Angeles: University of California Press, 1994).

27. See chapter 5 for more detailed discussion of my use of the term "intertext."

age and packing plants which Western enterprise has erected at various ports.

We pushed on. "The river wound so much that its course went round the compass," to quote Ellis again. Hills rose from either shore, their grassy banks were studded with groups of trees and temples were perched wherever a glorious view could be obtained. Some distance South of Ta Tung (Great Permeation), lies Chiu Hua Shan (Nine Flowers Mountain), so named by Li T'ai-po who is said to have likened the peaks . . . to the upturned petals of a lotus flower. (140–41)

As befits the genre of literary tourism, other travelers on the same routes quoted Ayscough's description of her trip only a few years later. Alice Tisdale Hobart, for instance, writes in her travelogue *Within the Walls of Nanking* (1928), to which Ayscough contributed "Proem,"

> As I stood at the rail with the docks drawing nearer, fragments of Florence Ayscough's description of Nanking passed through my mind. She had stood like this imagining she saw ghostly figures, Nanking's past rulers, famous beauties, poets, scholars, painters . . . endless ancient footsteps, many reminders of glorious and prosperous epochs in the history of Nanking, but, said Mrs. Ayscough, "I seem to have heard more about the sadness, the tragedies and the strifes which have taken place both within and without the walls."[28]

Such a web of cross-reference is created, however, not merely for encapsulating travel experiences, but more important, just as is often seen in Chinese travel writing where the narrator cites other texts to inscribe himself into historiography and history, Ayscough's quotations and allusions also provide a space for social and cultural commentary. As she quotes again from the British diplomat Henry Ellis, who described his travel in the same area with a sense of disgust, Ayscough inserts her own

---

28. Alice Tisdale Hobart, *Within the Walls of Nanking* (London: Jonathan Cape, 1928), 85.

critique: "To us, a century later, his attitude of mind is necessarily difficult to grasp, but making all allowance for inevitable ignorance, it is almost impossible to pardon the complacent superiority with which Occidentals set out to establish relations with countries which had no desire whatever for their presence" (142).

If I may be allowed a moment of self-reflection, I want to stress that, in the current volume, which is very much about my own journey through these writings about Asia, I quote extensively from the authors—and from their quotations from other texts—not simply in order to replicate the intertextual mechanism that has produced the works I study. More important, I quote in order to detail a complicated textual history that will enable me, I hope, to engage discursively with my fellow travelers who have often refused to enter into this textual landscape. To be sure, to those who believe that any textualization of the Other will necessarily contain a grain of cultural imperialism, the difference between a Henry Ellis, who textualizes the Other with utter ignorance, and a Florence Ayscough, who textualizes the Other with some genuine interest, may be inconsequential. But I would argue that when an author is interested in a literary culture to such an extent that, as we see in Ayscough, she has even incorporated part of that tradition into her text, interpretations based on a positivistic history that may be logically coherent or even politically sound badly need revising. I agree completely with my fellow travelers that these textual incorporations or appropriations—what Greenblatt has called, in a different context, "marvelous possessions"—should be subject to closer scrutiny for their ideological contents. Yet, I am also interested to see how these possessions become agents of dispossession, how the new discourses, whose very makeup derives from these appropriations, reshape the cultural reality from which they emerged.

The appropriation of part of the textual culture when one writes ethnographically about that culture in general—I will continue to develop this motif in my study. Especially in the next few chapters on Imagism, I demonstrate the ways in which poets Ezra Pound and Amy

Lowell have drawn upon the ethnographic work of P. Lowell, Fenollosa, and Ayscough and replicated the process of linguistic appropriation. The poets have poeticized their predecessors' prosaic descriptions of Oriental linguistic landscapes, descriptions that are often deemed in comparative poetics to be merely "source materials." What the Imagists have intertextually created, I argue, is their own ethnography about the Orient.

TWO

Ezra Pound

An Ideographer or Ethnographer?

Direct treatment of the "thing" whether subjective or
objective.

Ezra Pound, "A Few Don'ts by an Imagiste"

When Ezra Pound wrote down the first of the three Imagistic principles,
as seen in the epigraph, he was of course playing cards at the table of
poetry rather than ethnography. What he meant by the "thing" was poetic
matter that lives mostly in one's imagination—an image. It really would be
far-fetched to claim that a poem like "In a Station of the Metro" is a
semantically ethnographic description of Oriental culture or race:

IN A STATION OF THE METRO

The apparition   of these faces   in the crowd   :
Petals   on a wet, black   bough   .[1]

In reality, "these faces in the crowd" were those that the poet saw in a
metro station in Paris. However, there is no mistake that this poem is

1. I am following the page layout of the first published version of the poem in *Poetry*
(Chicago) in 1913, a version that is now reprinted in Ezra Pound, *Personae* (New York: New
Directions, 1990), 251.

stylistically an imitation of Japanese *haiku*, and styles of poetry or features of language, as we have seen in the preceding chapter, often become registers of cultural traits. In this chapter, I reinterpret one significant aspect of Pound's work on Chinese materials, an aspect that should be characterized as quintessentially ethnographic.

To understand the Imagist Pound as an ethnographer of Asia, at least three things must be clear: first, the difference between what a poem says and what a poem does; second, the intricate intertextual relationship that an Imagistic poem, such as "In a Station of the Metro," maintains with the extensive body of ethnographies produced by the poet's predecessors and contemporaries; third, a redefinition of the anthropological term *field*.

According to the authors of the speech-act theory, namely J. L. Austin and John R. Searle, the act of discourse is achieved on three levels: (1) the level of the locutionary or propositional act, the act of saying; (2) the level of the illocutionary act or force, what the speaker does in saying; (3) the level of the perlocutionary act, what the speakers do by the fact that they speak. If I tell you to close the door, I do three things: First, I relate the action predicate (to close) to two variables (you and the door)—this is the act of saying; second, I tell you this with the force of an order rather than a statement, wish, or promise—this is the illocutionary act; and finally, I provoke consequences such as fear by the fact that I give you an order—this is the perlocutionary act.

Although writing is not equal to speech, it can, as Paul Ricoeur explains, be exteriorized as discourse and thereby obtain the same three speech-act functions: the locutionary act of writing is exteriorized in the sentence qua proposition; the illocutionary act can be exteriorized by means of grammatical paradigms (the moods: indicative, imperative, conditional, and subjunctive) and other procedures that "mark" the illocutionary force of a sentence; and the perlocutionary act is a function that speech and writing actually share.[2] This application of the speech-

2. Paul Ricoeur, *Hermeneutics and the Human Sciences*, ed. and trans. John B. Thompson (Cambridge: Cambridge University Press, 1981), 134–35.

act theory to writing creates a possibility to read a poem not only for its locutionary, or semantic, values but also for its illocutionary and per-locutionary—that is, performative—values. It enables interpretation of a poem for what it does as well as for what it says. And one thing that an Imagistic poem does, I argue, is project an image of Asia by means of linguistic appropriation and reinvention.

But the Imagists seldom appropriated directly from linguistic cultures of which they had very little first-hand knowledge; instead, they relied intertextually on the work of other ethnographers. And this intertextual relation characterizes the remarkable trajectories of what I call transpacific displacement, the meandering routes of transpacific migration of cultural meanings. Here I understand intertextuality as a state in which multiple texts or versions of a text are interdependent and in which one text appropriates and/or distantiates others. Or, as Julia Kristeva puts it, following Mikhail Bakhtin, "Any text is the absorption and transformation of another."[3] In this sense, Imagism can be understood as an ethnography based on the matter of intertexts: the production of "image" and meaning in Imagism takes place in its intertextual relation to other poetries and ethnographies. Imagism, in other words, exists in a much wider world of intertexts.

Furthermore, to read Imagistic poems as ethnography or to regard Pound as an ethnographer, we also need to redefine a key term in anthropology—*field*. Fieldwork, as a traditional requirement for any institutionalized ethnographer, demarcates anthropology from competing disciplines. The work entails spending time physically dwelling among the "Others," pitching a tent in the "village," and collecting data by means of participant-observation. But, as James Clifford points out, this has not always been the case for ethnography:

> Prior to Boas, Malinowski, Mead, Firth, et al., the anthropological scholar usually remained at home, processing ethnographic informa-

3. Julia Kristeva, *The Kristeva Reader*, ed. Toril Moi (New York: Columbia University Press, 1986), 37.

tion sent by "men on the spot" who were drawn from among the sojourners just mentioned [i.e., explorers, missionaries, colonial officers, traders, colonists, and natural scientific researchers]. . . . Whatever exceptions there may have been to this pattern, interactive depth and co-residence were not yet professional requirements.[4]

It was only with the founding of cultural anthropology by Boas and his followers in the early decades of the twentieth century that fieldwork became the core of the discipline. Yet, this seemingly indispensable requirement is now being questioned by the new turns made in ethnography in the milieu of postmodernism. Starting with *Writing Culture: The Poetics and Politics of Ethnography*, edited by James Clifford and George Marcus (1986), a book that has fundamentally changed the perspective on anthropological work, critical attention has been shifted to a concern with the textual strategies used in the writing of ethnography. Consequently, "fieldwork" takes on new meanings that might transgress the old disciplinary definition.

One example of such new meaning can be found in Clifford's *Routes*. With the aim to question "how cultural analysis constitutes its objects . . . in spatial terms and through specific spatial practices of research" and to "reroute" the field by advocating a multilocality of fields, Clifford investigates travel and translation as cases of anthropological practice in which the ethnographer no longer settles down in a Malinowskian tent pitched in the center of a "village." These two terms, he claims, point to the shifting routes / roots and multiple locales where the ethnographic work can take place (17–46, 52–91).

Yet, Clifford, as well as other postmodern anthropologists, is not willing to go so far as to recognize another field for ethnographic work—the field of the text.[5] Text is probably the "final frontier" of anthropology as a disci-

4. James Clifford, *Routes: Travel and Translation in the Late Twentieth Century* (Cambridge: Harvard University Press, 1997), 64.

5. Clifford Geertz perhaps comes closest in recognizing text as a legitimate "field" for anthropology. See his *Interpretation of Cultures* (New York: BasicBooks, 1973) and *Works and Lives: The Anthropologist as Author* (Stanford: Stanford University Press, 1988).

pline, for beyond that, anthropology may not be distinguishable from cultural studies or literary criticism. But anthropology's "existential fear" of losing its disciplinary self should not prevent ethnographers from claiming the territory shared by anthropology and literature, the territory crucial to the investigation of Imagism as modern ethnography. After all, not only have the collecting, interpreting, translating, editing, and publishing of texts been at the core of cultural and linguistic anthropological work, but ethnography based on textual research, or, as called by a euphemism, "anthropology at a distance," has been a common practice among anthropologists. Ruth Benedict's *The Chrysanthemum and the Sword: Patterns of Japanese Culture* (1946) is a salient example of this. Benedict had never been to Japan to do any fieldwork in the conventional sense; her immensely popular wartime ethnography on the country was thus worked out *intertextually*, that is, by appropriating other texts.

The relocation of *field* in the textual world may have violated the boundary sanctioned by the discipline of anthropology, but the apparent transgression has profound philosophical implications. I have in mind what Ricoeur has called "the world of the text." Drawing on Martin Heidegger's redefinition of "understanding" as a structure of being-in-the-world, Ricoeur retains the idea of "the projection of our ownmost possibilities" in understanding and applies it to the theory of the text, suggesting that "what must be interpreted in a text is a *proposed world* which I could inhabit and wherein I could project one of my ownmost possibilities" (*Hermeneutics* 142). He further maintains that the text is much more than a particular case of intersubjective communication: it is the paradigm of distanciation in communication. As such, it displays a fundamental characteristic of the very historicity of human experience, namely that it is communication in and through distance (131).

When the text is regarded as that that enables us to communicate at a distance, the intertextual relations become all the more important because they become a necessary continuation or extension of our experiences. Therefore, we should expand Ricoeur's notion and propose a world of intertexts, one in which dialogues and cross-references among texts constitute the "very historicity" of our efforts to know the world, to comprehend the meaning of the Other, and to project "our ownmost possibilities"— efforts that characterize the ostensible goals of the "science of humankind."

With the relocation of the anthropological *field* in the world of inter-texts, I now turn to the work of the Imagist Pound and consider the inter-textual means by which he created a modernist ethnography. I shall focus on his textual encounter with Asia, his editing of Fenollosa's manuscript, and his giant pancultural program centered on the idea of *paideuma*.

Ezra Pound (1885–1972) never stepped onto Asian soil, although he had a lifelong craving for Confucian culture, and he was an avid traveler. His earliest encounter with the Far East came from his frequent visits to the British Museum in London and from his reading various books on Chi-nese literature. During his early years in London, Pound was intro-duced to Chinese and Japanese painting by Laurence Binyon, an En-glish poet who was then working as assistant keeper of the Department of Prints and Drawings in the British Museum. The department housed and exhibited Asian paintings, some of which were of extremely high artistic and market value. The role that museums played in modern Western art and literature has been studied quite extensively.[6] African and other "aboriginal" arts that usually came through museum collec-tions not only influenced modernist painting but also inspired literary modernism, as evidenced in the work of Gertrude Stein, W. B. Yeats, T. S. Eliot, and many others. Pound was no exception.

But "influence" and "inspiration," terms often used in traditional comparative poetics, are not precise in describing the cross-cultural encounter. In Pound's case, especially, his encounter with the Far East by way of the paintings in the British Museum should be understood in terms of what Roman Jakobson has called the *transmutation*. In the essay

6. Two examples are James Clifford, *The Predicament of Culture: Twentieth-Century Ethnography, Literature, and Art* (Cambridge: Harvard University Press, 1988), and Elazar Barkan and Ronald Bush, eds., *Prehistories of the Future: The Primitivist Project and the Culture of Modernism* (Stanford: Stanford University, 1995).

"Linguistic Aspects of Translation," linguist and literary theoretician Jakobson suggests that there are three kinds of translation: intralingual translation (rewording), interlingual translation (translation proper), and intersemiotic translation (transmutation). He defines the last one as "an interpretation of verbal signs by means of signs of nonverbal sign systems."[7] But here I think "transmutation" should also be applicable to the reverse intersemiotic process, that is, an interpretation of nonverbal signs by means of verbal signs.

What the Chinese paintings provided Pound were essentially visual texts that he had to interpret, and his interpretation was transmutational in the sense that he understood them by producing poetic, intersemiotic versions of these paintings. *Admonitions of the Instructress to Court Ladies*, a Han (206 B.C.–220 A.D.) masterpiece, is "made up of nine visually stunning scenes, each illustrating a quotation from a Han text dealing with correct court conduct."[8] The second scene, in particular, represents a Han imperial concubine, Ban Jieyu, " 'refusing the Emperor's invitation to ride with him in his palanquin' for fear of distracting him from state affairs" (Qian 13). Later, the poem, "Fan-Piece for Her Imperial Lord," appeared in Pound's 1914 anthology, *Des Imagistes*:

> O fan of white silk,
>> clear as frost on the grass-blade,
> You also are laid aside. (45)

Better still, even this act of Jakobsonian transmutation was not completely Pound's creation, for the triplet was adapted from one of Ban Jieyu's poems translated by H. A. Giles in *A History of Chinese Literature* (1901):

7. Roman Jakobson, *Language in Literature* (Cambridge: Harvard University Press, 1987), 429.

8. Zhaoming Qian, *Orientalism and Modernism* (Durham: Duke University Press, 1995), 13.

O fair white silk, fresh from the weaver's loom,
Clear as the frost, bright as the winter snow—
See! friendship fashions out of thee a fan,
Round as the round moon shines in heaven above,
At home, abroad, a close companion thou,
Stirring at every move the grateful gale.
And yet I fear, ah me! that autumn chills,
Cooling the dying summer's torrid rage,
Will see thee laid neglected on the shelf,
All thought of bygone days, like them bygone.[9]

Comparing Giles's version with Pound's "Fan-Piece," Zhaoming Qian, to whom I am greatly indebted for the admirably detailed documentation in his work, has this to say about Pound's imitation of *haiku*: "Pound had experimented with the Japanese form in other poems, but this appears to be more like a genuine *haiku*. Not only has it followed the 5-7-5 syllabic pattern more rigorously, but it has an authentic Far Eastern content" (46). I, however, doubt the "authenticity" that Poundian scholars of the last three decades have been attributing to his work in light of comparative poetics.[10]

Allen Upward, who initially introduced Pound to Giles's work, offers a clue regarding the manufacture of the "authenticity." In the September 1913 issue of *Poetry*, Upward published a sequence of poems entitled "Scented Leaves from a Chinese Jar." They immediately caught Pound's attention because they were reminiscent of his own experience with those Chinese paintings in the British Museum. Soon Pound found out about Upward's method of composition: "[Upward] made it up out of his head, using a certain amount of Chinese reminiscence" (qtd. in

9. H. A. Giles, *A History of Chinese Literature* (New York: D. Appleton, 1901), 101.

10. See Hugh Kenner, *The Pound Era* (Berkeley and Los Angeles: University of California Press, 1971); Wai-Lim Yip, *Ezra Pound's* Cathay (Princeton: Princeton University Press, 1969); Beongcheon Yu, *The Great Circle: American Writers and the Orient* (Detroit: Wayne State University Press, 1983); Sanehide Kodama, *American Poetry and Japanese Culture* (Hamden, Conn.: Archon Books, 1984); and Qian, *Orientalism and Modernism* (1995).

Qian, 20). But Pound did not realize that the "certain amount of Chinese reminiscence" was in fact a paraphrase, or rather, a Jakobsonian intralingual translation. Upward did not simply make it up "out of his head," as he would confirm a few years later in a verse letter:

> In the year nineteen hundred a poet named Granmer Byng
> brought to my attic in Whitehall Gardens a book of
> Chinese Gems by Professor Giles,
> Eastern butterflies coming there into my attic beside
> the Stygian Thames,
> And read me one of them—willows, forsaken young wife,
> spring.
> Immediately my soul kissed the soul of immemorial China[11]

It is evident that the "Chinese reminiscence" came out of Upward's reading, or rather his poet-friend Granmer Byng's reading, of Giles's translation. But neither "reminiscence" nor "paraphrase" can sufficiently illustrate a significant intertextual strategy; it is a strategy that Robert Kern has called "re-orientalization." In *Orientalism, Modernism, and the American Poem* (1996), Kern argues that Imagists both modernized Orientalism and orientalized Modernism, and that to achieve the former, they reorientalized the old Orientalism manifest in the previous translations (James Legge, Giles, etc.) by making the text sound more "oriental."[12]

Following Kern's acute observation, I emphasize the intertextual strategy that has made the reorientalization possible. Both Upward's sequence and Pound's "Fan-Piece," which revised and reorientalized the Chinese texts, were based on their readings of works by Giles and others. What has often been understood in the banal sense of "study of sources" should, as Kristeva suggests, be called by "transposition," a term indicating that "the passage from one signifying system to another demands a

11. Quotation from J. B. Harmer, *Victory in Limbo: Imagism 1908–1917* (London: Secker & Warburg, 1975), 137.

12. Robert Kern, *Orientalism, Modernism, and the American Poem* (Cambridge: Cambridge University Press, 1996), 189.

new articulation."[13] Reorientalization is, therefore, an intertextual transposition carried out in various shifting contact zones, including museums, paintings, translations, readings, and poetic re-creations.[14] These zones are potential fields along the transpacific routes where intertextual (re)makings of culture constantly take place. This transpositional process can be demonstrated more clearly in the second stage of Pound's textual encounter with the Far East—his editing and reworking of Fenollosa's manuscript, which resulted in the publications of *Cathay* in 1915 and *The Chinese Written Character as a Medium for Poetry* in 1918.

In 1913, five years after Fenollosa's sudden death, his widow, Mary Fenollosa, found the young poet Pound and entrusted him with Fenollosa's papers. If Pound's earlier flirtation with Chinese poetry was only transposing popular versions of translation into his Imagistic poems, at this stage, as the literary executor of the eminent American Orientalist, he had much more credibility in fashioning a new face for Chinese poetry and thereby promoting his modernist poetics. However, it would be a grave error to assume that Pound's interest was only in poetry. It

13. Julia Kristeva, *Revolution in Poetic Language*, trans. Margaret Waller (New York: Columbia University Press, 1984), 111.

14. In *Imperial Eyes: Travel and Transculturation* (London: Routledge, 1992), Mary Louise Pratt defines the "contact zone" as "the space of colonial encounters, the space in which peoples geographically and historically separated come into contact with each other and establish ongoing relations, usually involving conditions of coercion, radical inequality, and intractable conflict" (6). But I am not using this term in a colonial context. An argument could be made, for instance, that Pound's encounter with Chinese art collected in the British Museum was made possible by the British invasion and colonization of China starting from the 1840 Opium War. Illegal smuggling and wartime looting had caused numerous treasures of Chinese art to mysteriously "disappear" from China and suddenly show up in the collection of the British Museum. For instance, a Han masterpiece entitled *Admonitions of the Instructress to Court Ladies*, which was seen by Pound and had also inspired him, was originally preserved in the Imperial Palace in Beijing. It was lost during the turmoil in 1900 when the palace was looted by the joint troops of Europe and the United States, and it subsequently appeared in the British Museum. But such recontextualization, albeit useful to some extent in putting Pound's poems into a positivistic historical perspective, contributes little to my main concern—that is, how Pound intertextually created an ethnography of Asia. The movement of the related texts and of the cultural meanings carried by them constitutes a *textual history* that remains my focus.

would be an even bigger mistake to regard his work on Chinese poetry as separable from the ethnographic interest that lies at the heart of Fenollosa's ambitious project. Indeed, Pound, who dreamt of becoming "lord of his work and master of utterance" (*Cantos* 442), was never merely—if I may coin a word to characterize someone who is enamored by ideograph and promotes the so-called ideogrammic method—an ideographer; he had always been an ethnographer.

When Pound claimed that he had corrected only a few words when editing Fenollosa's *CWC*, he might have spoken with a grain of truth if he were referring to those stylistic glosses that had made the article itself sound more "Imagistic." Given the fact that Impressionism was one of the targets Imagism was attacking, reshaping Fenollosa's somewhat Impressionistic verbiage into Pound's Imagistic precision seemed to be quite appropriate. Compare this original passage by Fenollosa

> He resolves its indifference with a thousand prismatic tints of highly colored verbs. His figures flood things with simultaneous jets of light, or of the sudden blaze of illuminated fountains. (B101 F4248)

with the new passage edited by Pound

> He resolves its indifference into a thousand tints of verb. His figures flood things with jets of various light, like the sudden up-blaze of fountains. (*CWC* 35)

Pound clearly applied the second rule of Imagism: "To use absolutely no word that does not contribute to the presentation."[15] As for poetry, so for prose.

However, Pound not only made the composition of the article Imagistic, but he also rendered the Chinese language and poetry in the article even more so. In the manuscript version of *CWC*, Fenollosa had used a nonidiomatic Chinese sentence, 日上東, to illustrate his "uni-

---

15. Ezra Pound, *Literary Essays of Ezra Pound*, ed. T. S. Eliot (London: Faber and Faber, 1954), 7.

versal grammar." But Pound apparently saw the possibility to improve the "vividness" of the illustration; therefore, a third "sun" dazzled into the sentence:

日　昇　東

This is the only version of the Chinese sentence known and commented upon by critics; but, this was not the original example that Fenollosa used in his manuscript (see fig. 3), and all evidence indicates that it was Pound who changed the second character.

I can find four places in Fenollosa's manuscript where 日上東 is written in Fenollosa's hand and another place where the passage is apparently referring to this "sentence." The four places are all located in the three volumes of "Chinese and Japanese Poetry: Synopsis of Lectures":

(1) B99 F4217, vol. 1, verso facing p. 12.
(2) B99 F4218, vol. 2, verso facing p. 39.
(3) B99 F4218, vol. 2, verso facing p. 50.
(4) B99 F4219, vol. 3, verso facing p. 10.

In B101 F4248, which contains the most complete version of *CWC* and which is also the one that Pound used for editing and publication, there is a previously mentioned passage that has no illustration but undoubtedly refers to 日上東:[16]

> Examples are strewn on every hand. To repeat one of the simplest—
> "The Sun rises in the East." Here sun, which already means "shin-
> ing" enters in the most picturesque way into the character for East,
> shining entangled in the branches of a tree. There is something daz-
> zling in the repetition, something like the concentrated rays that
> come from diamonds. Moreover, there is homology between the
> upright line of the rising, and the upright growing line of the tree. If

16. This passage can also be found in B99 F4219, vol. 3, p. 10, which is the fourth place the Chinese illustration appears.

we should add an horizon line across the roots of the tree, the sun would just take the place of the dot in the second character.

The explanation regarding the sun taking the place of the dot sounds far-fetched, and Pound might have been dissatisfied with it. What could he do to make the sentence more "picturesque" and more "Chinese"? Maybe change the character! After all, 昇 easily available in Robert Morrison's *A Dictionary of the Chinese Language*, which Pound was using at the time, and it does mean "(sun) rise."

Moreover, Fenollosa's manuscript has at least seventeen plates of Chinese calligraphy to be used as illustrations in *CWC*, and one of the plates is 日上東. These seventeen plates are pasted onto thin rice paper, and one of them has Fenollosa's annotation on it; hence, there is no doubt that these are Fenollosa's plates and his version was 日上東. In the same folder, there is now another plate, which is a duplication of Fenollosa's version, pasted onto a piece of paper with the letterhead "Rapallo"—an emblem of our own Ez (B101 F4245). Therefore, it should be a reasonable speculation that Pound started out with Fenollosa's version, but then changed his mind and adopted a "better" one. Consequently, we now have this conclusion reworded by Pound along with a recharactered example:

> Here also the Chinese ideography has its advantage, in even a simple line; for example, "The sun rises in the east."
>
> The overtones vibrate against the eye. The wealth of composition in characters makes possible a choice of words in which a single dominant overtone colors every plane of meaning. That is perhaps the most conspicuous quality of Chinese poetry. Let us examine our line.

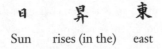

日　　昇　　東
Sun　rises (in the)　east

The sun, the shining, on one side, on the other the sign of the east, which is the sun entangled in the branches of a tree. And in the middle sign, the verb "rise," we have further homology; the sun is above the horizon, but beyond that the single upright line is like the growing trunk-line of the tree sign. This is but a beginning, but it points a way to the method, and to the method of intelligent reading. (*CWC* 36–37)

Compared with Fenollosa's original passage, this new version runs much more smoothly, the homology is much more striking, and the Chinese sounds much more "Chinese." The efficaciousness should be attributed not merely to what Pound, in the added last sentence, calls the "intelligent reading," but also to what I understand as intertextual transposition, which entails quoting, paraphrasing, revising, and at times, exaggerating by means of invented examples.

While critics have pointed out that exaggerations, fabrications, and misattributions constitute an indispensable part of Pound's "poetics of errors," Pound's character substitution in this case actually contains another twist that should be regarded as a very revealing and significant step in transpacific textual migrations.[17] It is commonly known that both Pound's and Fenollosa's understandings of the visualness of the Chinese character are results of a misperception. But it is, to be sure, a misperception attributable not completely to Pound or Fenollosa. There exists a deeply rooted Western conception of "pictorial" Chinese, a conception that dates back to the Renaissance. But in this particular case, Pound's and Fenollosa's misperception may also have been caused by a mediating factor that is often ignored in transpacific studies, a missing link between the Chinese and the American—that is, the mediation by Japanese interpretations.

Japanese nationalist discourse and the concomitant interpretation of the "foreign" origin of Chinese characters have given shape to Fenollosa's studies. But the Japanese influence does not stop there; in fact, with its ascending status in the eyes of the West after the Russo-

17. See Christine Froula, *To Write Paradise: Style and Error in Pound's Cantos* (New Haven: Yale University Press, 1984). Froula argues that the *Cantos* "enacts the constitutive status of error in modern history as it plays out its implications for poetic form" (dust jacket).

Japanese war, Japan became almost a spokesperson for the much weaker China and Korea—a fact that Fenollosa and many of his fellow travelers readily acknowledged.[18] In the study of Chinese poetry, Japanese interpretations have also been accepted by the West as the standard if not simply the best. But the methodologies adopted by Japanese scholars of Chinese poetry have often produced what seems to me a defamiliarized version of Chinese that foregrounds the characters' iconicity rather than their phoneticity. One example of such methodology is *wakun*, the Japanese method of reading Chinese that was popular for centuries. According to Naoki Sakai, whose monumental study of Japanese language theories I draw on here, *wakun* is formed by "putting markers and Japanese particles in the margins of Chinese characters," and the outcome of this transformation is that any reading of Chinese will have to be "undertaken visually, or at least with reference to visual signs."[19] Sakai provides an example of *wakun*. A Chinese passage such as

譯之一字。爲讀書眞訣。蓋書皆文字。文字即華人語言。

should be vocalized in Mandarin Chinese as *"Yi zhi yizi, wei dushu zhenjue, gai shu jie wenzi, wenzi ji huaren yuyan."* But Japanese scholars using

18. For Fenollosa's acknowledgment of this fact, see chapter 1. Florence Ayscough made a similar point in her essay "Written Pictures": "We are deeply indebted to the Japanese for all that they have done to make the whole subject [of Chinese art and language] comprehensible." But Ayscough was quick to add that "We must never forget that in accepting their [the Japanese] opinions and their renditions we are accepting those of a people alien to the Chinese, a people who differ widely in their philosophy, their temperament, and their ideals; a people who, although they have borrowed the ideographs of the Chinese have, in many cases, modified and altered the original meanings" (271–72). Perhaps it is worth noting that Ayscough's simultaneous acknowledgment and skepticism was quite self-serving: she was alluding to and trying to undermine a competing project on Chinese poetry that relies openly on Japanese interpretations—that is, the Fenollosa/Pound project. Ayscough's essay was an introduction to the Chinese poems she and Amy Lowell had cotranslated that appeared in the February 1919 issue of *Poetry* (Chicago). Pound's *Cathay* was published in 1915 to astonishing critical acclaim, and Fenollosa's essay on the Chinese character, edited by Pound, was due to appear in *The Little Review* later in 1919.

19. Naoki Sakai, *Voices of the Past: The Status of Language in Eighteenth-Century Japanese Discourse* (Ithaca: Cornell University Press, 1991), 225.

the *wakun* method added marks and particles and produced a passage as follows:

諸之｜字°爲‖讀書 讀訟 ，°蓋 書皆文字 ‖‵。文字即挿人 ‵語言 ‵。

The new passage is vocalized as *"Yaku no ichiji, dokusho no shinketsu tari, kedashi sho wa mina monji ni shite, monji wa sunawachi kajin no gogen nari"* (*Voices* 227).

Sakai writes that words such as *shinketsu* or *gogen* "are phonetic imitations of the Chinese original and cannot be understood by the general readership unless the visual text ... is referred to" (ibid.). A comparison between Sakai's example and a page from Fenollosa's notes taken when he was studying Chinese poetry with the Japanese masters (see figs. 4 and 7) shows that the two are strikingly similar in their use of the *wakun* form. As the notes show, Fenollosa was learning to vocalize Chinese poems by means of Japanese phonetics. Given that *wakun* is an imperfect form of reading Chinese and is always dependent on a visual text, it makes perfect sense, I suppose, that Fenollosa and Pound would go on to promulgate the visualness of Chinese characters at the expense of the phonetic. It then becomes clear that what has always seemed to be a misreading by Fenollosa and by Pound is actually attributable to a peculiar style of translingual interpretation practiced by Japanese scholars.[20] The whole process exemplifies, to be sure, an instance of textual migration that has remarkable implications for cultural descriptions.

Whereas following a foreign tradition of interpreting a third linguistic culture may produce one version of "misreading," imposing one's own interpretive frame upon a foreign text will surely lead, for better or worse, to another version of "misrepresentation." If, in the editing of

20. Lydia Liu (*Translingual Practice: Literature, National Culture, and Translated Modernity—China, 1900–1937* [Stanford: Stanford University Press, 1995]) and others have argued eloquently that in the early modern period, Japan functioned almost as a distributor of Western ideologies in East Asia. I suggest that Japan was also a key exporter of Asian cultural meanings to the West, as evidenced in the literary interactions I am describing.

Fenollosa's essay, Pound's transposition involves just changing a few
Chinese characters and making them appear more visual, then in *Cathay*
Pound seems to be conducting cosmetic surgery upon the face of the
Chinese text. When *Cathay* was published in 1915, Pound made it clear
on the title page that the small book of twelve (in fact, thirteen) poems
was made "for the most part . . . from the notes of the late Ernest Fenollosa, and the decipherings of the professors Mori and Ariga." However,
Pound was in fact carrying out a very different poetic and textual practice from that of Fenollosa, or Mori and Ariga, or ultimately, from that
of the Chinese.

The Chinese text is the point of departure of the transpacific journey.
There is one aspect of the Chinese that Pound and most of his followers have either refused to recognize or simply blocked out of their imagination: The Chinese are not always a people "close to nature" when it
comes to linguistic practice. Indeed, the Chinese have fashioned a textual tradition that cherishes scrupulous, at times even seemingly
tedious, annotation as a companion to their "close-to-nature" poetry.[21]
To make it worse, the poetry and its intimate companion are very often
printed neck to neck on the page, with poetry lines being ruthlessly
interrupted by the annotation. See a page from *The Complete Works of Li
Po*, a poem that appeared in *Cathay* as "The River Song" (see fig. 5).

The page should be read vertically, from the right to the left. The
characters in larger font are the poetry lines while the ones in smaller
font are intersecting annotations—notes upon notes, commentaries
upon commentaries. The many different labels attached to these annotations should indicate their significance to the hermeneutics of Chinese texts: An initial explanation of the primary text is called *zhu* or *shi;*
a second-level explanation of the primary text and/or of the initial
explanation is called *shu,* or *zhengyi;* further down, *jie, jiao, tong, quan,
shuyi, jiaoshu, quanshi, ping, dian,* and so on—all refer to different kinds

---

21. It is a tradition of textual practice comparable to the Talmudic one, something that
Pound openly despised.

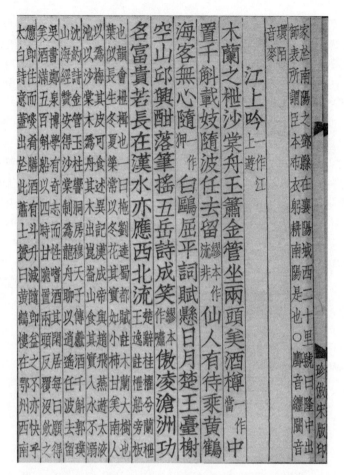

5. Li Po, "Jiang Shang Yin" (The river song). Reproduced from a facsimile version of a Sung (960–1279) edition of *Li Taibai Shi Quanji* (The complete poems of Li Po).

and levels of annotations. Interestingly enough, as in the case of "Jiang Shang Yin" (The river song), the endless cross-reference is not printed separately from the poetry lines; instead, they intersect the lines, insisting on their own existence. In such a textual environment, the authoritative status of the poetry lines becomes questionable.

Fenollosa's notes from Mori's tutorial sessions did not deviate too far from such a Chinese textual practice, for the Japanese carried on the Chinese tradition. But a major break came about when Pound took over the notes and worked out his "Chinese invention." The apparent difference lies between the symbiosis of poetry and annotation in Fenollosa and the lack of annotation (except for two paraphrasing items) in Pound. Now the question boils down to this: Does a poem stand by itself?

There are some enlightening moments in *Cathay* that have caused much controversy among critics. One such moment came when Pound, adapting "The River Song" by Rihaku (Li Po) from Fenollosa's notes, mistakenly conflated two poems into one. The long title of another poem that follows immediately, "Poem Composed at the Command of the Emperor in I-Chun Park on the Dragon-Pond as the Willows Are in Their Fresh Green and the New Orioles Are Singing in Their Thousand Ways," in Pound's hand became part of "The River Song":

And I have moped in the Emperor's garden,
    awaiting an order-to-write!
I looked at the dragon-pond, with its willow-
    coloured water
Just reflecting the sky's tinge,
And heard the five-score nightingales aim-
    lessly singing. (*Cathay* 9)

Whereas Sinologists such as Arthur Waley and Achilles Fang simply jeered at such a "gross mistake," scholars of American High Modernism have defended Pound in the name of his poetic achievements.[22] It is legend now how Pound, the Great Master of Modernism, grasped the essence of these two poems, used his modernist "super-pository technique," and moved the two together as if they were "the two halves of a seal" (*Cantos* 467).

22. See Kenner, *Pound Era*; Yip, *Ezra Pound's* Cathay; Kodama, *American Poetry*, and Qian, *Orientalism and Modernism*.

Hugh Kenner, in particular, accounts for the "incidental mistake" in this way:

> This came about because Fenollosa kept the left-hand pages of the "Rihaku" notebooks for comments by Professor Mori. Three right-hand pages of "River Song" face three left-hand pages of comment; then a blank left-hand page faces the long title of a new poem about Li Po in the garden full of spring softness. Pound mistook this for more of "The River Song," and the blank left-hand page, which signals a new poem, for absence of comment by Mori. (204)

And Kenner is quick to play down the mistake, as he immediately writes:

> A surprisingly large number of the "errors" are quite deliberate. Chinese poets, practising an art which thrives, as did Pope's, on minimal variations within a tradition, summon up the tradition by constant allusion. Mori's notes normally explicated such matters. Pound, whose readers would see only 14 poems, very deftly worked his way round them, avoiding notes. (204–5)

To Kenner and others, the superiority of Pound's poetic genius over Fenollosa's annotative scholarship is all too obvious, and Pound's talent of recuperating the essence of Chinese poetry from Fenollosa's "unpoetic" notes remains indisputable. Commenting on the different aesthetic effects created by Fenollosa's transcription and by Pound's translation of a poem by Tao Chien ("To-Em-Mei"), Kenner asserts: "'To-Em-Mei,' as transcribed by Fenollosa, contains nothing of this [i.e., Pound's kind of poeticity].... Pound has unified the poem, obligated by a diction and a movement that expect unity, and done so by imposing on the notes just three distortions" (212).

This defense of Pound's "incidental errors" is based on a preconceived demarcation between poetry and annotation. Such a demarcation also lies at the core of Pound's poetics. Despite the fact that the Chinese poems in Fenollosa's notes cannot stand by themselves without the companionship of the various layers of annotations, Pound, by pushing aside all the notes, advocated a poetics that claims to abstract poeticity from a hybridized, dialogic (inter)textuality and perpetuated the autonomy and monologism of poetry itself. He not only transposed Fenollosa's "transliteration" but also reconstituted the textuality, intensifying the "Luminous Detail" and eradicating those "multitudinous details," managing to invent a Chinese poetry that represented the apex of Imagism's achievements in 1915.[23] And in doing so, Pound signed himself onto the list of ethnographers who did not plow the field of texts but plucked the fruits that were, as Dennis Tedlock puts it, "already there." In *The Spoken Word and the Work of Interpretation* (1983), Tedlock points out a pitfall in the ethnographer's dealing with texts from other cultures. He criticizes many ethnographers' practice of distinguishing between a "telling" about a story and a "doing" of a story, leaving interpretation up to themselves and narrative to the natives. "The collected texts are treated," Tedlock remarks, "as if they were raw products, to which value is then added by manufacture" (237). Pound's *Cathay* in effect carries out such a practice; it abstracts what is "poetry" from the cluster of "raw products"—notes—leaving out almost all the interpretation delivered in what Pound had mocked as "Mr. Mori's very simple and 'childish' language" (B99 F4222). If only Pound had cared to read a bit more carefully Mori's commentaries in Fenollosa's notebooks, he could have avoided the mistake of conflating two poems as well as many other errors in *Cathay*.

But Pound was not alone in stumbling over the notes; many scholars have shared this carelessness when it comes to dealing with annotations. Regarding Pound's mistake in "The River Song," critics after Kenner have tried to offer their own explanations. Sanehide Kodama, for one,

23. In "I Gather the Limbs of Osiris," now published in *Selected Prose* (ed. William Cookson [London: Faber and Faber, 1973]), Pound advocates a method "which has been intermittently used by all good scholars since the beginning of scholarship, the method of Luminous Detail, a method most vigorously hostile to the prevailing mode of today—that is, the method of multitudinous detail, and to the method of yesterday, the method of sentiment and generalisation" (21).

claims that "at the end of the first poem, Fenollosa comments, 'having come to conclusion,' suggesting that it is the end of the poem" (85). In his recent work, *Orientalism and Modernism* (1995), Zhaoming Qian attempts to correct Kodama: "In my repeated examinations of the notes in question, I have failed to locate the phrase, 'having come to conclusion.'" Nonetheless, Qian agrees with Kodama's assumption that "Pound, at his first hasty reading...confused the two poems" and that "by the time he got to serious work on them, he...was trying deliberately to make one poem out of two in the form of superposition" (195).

However, the phrase "having come to conclusion," which Qian failed to locate, is right there. Neither is Kodama correct, for the phrase is not "at" the end of the first poem but "toward" the end, and it does not at all suggest that "it is the end of the poem." In Fenollosa's notebook, corresponding to the poetry lines on the right, the commentary on the left says, "Moral—having come to conclusion that lit. fame is better than earthy, he is now merry. So, at height, he writes strong characters, and in them writes out this new poem made, and laughs beating with pride at having made an eternal thing" (see figs. 6, 7, 8, and 9).

It is obvious that the phrase "having come to conclusion" refers only to the corresponding two lines (*"Kio kwan raku hitsu yo go gaku/shi sei sho go rio so shu"*) and does not indicate the conclusion of the poem itself, because the poem has two more lines, which have their corresponding commentary. If Kodama had really taken the left-hand page notes seriously (which he did not transcribe in his book, whereas he did the right-hand page poetry), he would have been able to find that on the previous page the left-hand commentary also contains the phrase "the moral is...".[24] Here again, "the moral" leads a paraphrase of the corresponding poetry lines. Hence the phrase "having come to conclusion" does not in any way indicate the ending of the poem.

It is uncanny that Pound made a mistake because of his dislike of annotations: his Emersonian transparent eyeball, which should have

24. See verso page facing p. 3 in Yale B101 F4236 ("Mori and Ariga Notebook," vol. 2).

6. Verso page facing p. 4 in Fenollosa's "Mori and Ariga Notebook," vol. 2. Reproduced from B101 F4236, Yale Collection of American Literature, Beinecke Rare Book and Manuscript Library.

7. Page 4 from Fenollosa's "Mori and Ariga Notebook," vol. 2. Reproduced from B101 F4236, Yale Collection of American Literature, Beinecke Rare Book and Manuscript Library.

technique of next two lines
Merriment and poem couple—<u>at height</u> and
<u>made out</u> (or completed) <u>drop pen</u> and <u>laugh</u>
<u>a pride</u> (not a strict pair in words, but in idea)
Cause to move and extend over; five peaks and blue seas
prevail

Moral—having come to conclusion that lit fame
is better than earthy, he is now merry. And so, at height,
he writes strong characters, and in them writes out this new
poem made, and laughs beating with pride at having made
an eternal thing.

repeating thoughts
If fame (or official merit) etc. were to be eternal,
this water will run backward
expressing impossibility

———————

They say this is very well planned, and
poetically thought out

8.   A transcript of figure 6, verso facing p. 4, as found in Fenollosa's notebook.

<u>kio</u>	<u>kwan</u>	<u>raku</u>	<u>hitsu</u>	<u>yo</u>	<u>go</u>	<u>gaku</u>
pleasure merriment	at its height	let fall brandished rapidly	pen	make move	five	peaks

At the height of the merriment, I sweep my pen, and write poems
in such powerful strokes as to cause the 5 peaks to tremble

<u>shi</u>	<u>sei</u>	<u>sho</u>	<u>go</u>	<u>rio</u>	<u>so</u>	<u>shu</u>
poem	is made	laugh	pride assume pride countenance (a verb)	compete with prevail	blue	a group of islands archipelago

The poem being now made, I laugh with new pride in my heart,
pride which spreads over (as wide as) the blue islands beyond

<u>ko</u>	<u>mei</u>	<u>fu</u>	<u>ki</u>	<u>jaku</u>	<u>cho</u>	<u>zai</u>
merit	fame	wealth	nobility	if	long	exist

If merit, fame, wealth, and nobility were to last for ever,

<u>Kan</u>	<u>Sui</u>	<u>yeki</u>	<u>o</u>	<u>sei</u>	<u>hoku</u>	<u>riu</u>
Kan name of the Kan ko Han River	water	also	will ought to	west	north	flow

The water of the Han River ought to flow North West (instead
of S.E., as now)

9. A transcript of figure 7, p. 4, as found in Fenollosa's notebook.

enabled him to behold "nature" in Chinese character and poetry, was somehow bewitched by the "unnatural" annotations, which he had chosen to exclude. The "unnatural" reassured its existence in the form of an error made by its terminator. It is even more uncanny that the Poundian scholars have thus deserted the tool of their trade, reconfirmed Pound's Volitionist literary ideology, and perpetuated the "unnatural" error.

To recall Tedlock's critique of ethnographers' practice of disregarding native interpretations that always come with the "stories" they are trying to collect, it is indeed in the same vein that Pound and other scholars have tried to "get the poetry" at the sacrifice of the annotation. But long before the ethnographers go to the natives' village to get the stories, Tedlock writes,

> Ashes and fire are already there together. In the live coal, the ashes and soot are not waiting to be projected by the fire. Elder and younger are already there. The Sun and the people are already there. Desire and possibility are already there. The word and the world are already there. The text and the interpretation are already there. (*Spoken* 246)

Indeed, Rihaku's two different poems are already there; Mori's comments are already there; Fenollosa's transcriptions are already there; the words "having come to conclusion" are already there; so are the morals . . .

Yet, getting the story or poetry does not represent the whole cultural project that Pound was pursuing. Just like Fenollosa, whose interest in Chinese poetry was led by an ethnographer's zeal to grasp the essence of "Chinese humanity" and of humanity in general, Pound integrated poetry into his giant program of culture, or *Kulchur*, as he called it. Having examined Pound's textual encounter with Chinese art and poetry in his early years and in his later work with Fenollosa's manuscript, I now turn to his broader ethnographic interest as manifested in the ensemble of his ideas, *Guide to Kulchur* (1938). The implications of three key concepts used in the book, *Kulchur, paideuma,* and *Kulturmorphologie* (transformation of culture), related to the work of German anthropologist Leo Frobenius, make Pound's role as a modern ethnographer clearer.

Pound regarded Leo Frobenius (1873–1938) as one of "the most intelligent men of the period" (*Guide* 217). Frobenius and Confucius were two of the cornerstones in Pound's cultural program. A German Diffusionist who tried to trace to "a common origin the whole culture of two remote areas, West Africa and Oceania" and to recover the lost glory of the legendary Atlantis, Frobenius was famed for his relentless effort in excavating bronze and terra-cotta heads in West Africa.[25] But all these archeological works and the huge collection of primitive arts, according to his biographer Janheinz Jahn, "were merely by-products... since they were to document his theory of culture."[26] Jahn summarizes Frobenius's cultural theory in this way:

> Cultures are to him living organisms, to begin with: "Culture lives and dies, arises anew and travels through cultural spaces on its own terms, as if man were not there, who indeed is only the tool for its formation." "Yet, culture has no legs. It takes it easy and lets itself be carried by man. Wherever it appears, man must have carried it." "Cultures live, give birth, and die." But Frobenius goes further than Oswald Spengler, the author of *Der Untergang des Abendlandes* [The Decline of the West]; he sees something behind culture: the "essence of culture." This essence in its turn has a soul: the *paideuma*. (13)

Pound had picked up this coinage, *paideuma*, in his reading of Frobenius's eight-volume *Erlebte Erdteile*. He compared the term to Confucius's CH'ENG MING 正名, or the New Learning (literally, the "cor-

---

25. Robert H. Lowie, *The History of Ethnological Theory* (New York: Rinehart, 1937), 159. It is interesting that Frobenius published his first anthropological work, *The Childhood of Man: A Popular Account of the Lives, Customs & Thoughts of the Primitive Races*, trans. A. H. Keane (London: Seeley, 1909), without having done any "fieldwork," but simply by collecting samples of primitive art and other writers' accounts of primitive life—another salient example of "anthropology at a distance."

26. Janheinz Jahn, *Leo Frobenius: The Demonic Child*, trans. Reinhard Sander (Austin: African and Afro-American Studies and Research Center of the University of Texas, 1974), 13.

rect naming"), and to Fenollosa's ideogrammic method. He traced Frobenius's neologism back to its Greek roots in *paideia*, or culture,[27] and entitled his textbook on civilization *Guide to Kulchur*, retaining the connotations of both German and African American vernacular in the key word. "When I said I wanted a new civilization," Pound wrote, "I think I cd. have used Frobenius' term" (*Guide* 58). Just as his adoption of African American vernacular constitutes an interesting ethnographic aspect of Pound's work, this German connotation is also crucial to the understanding of the anthropological nature of Pound's cultural program.[28]

According to Raymond Williams, the English word "culture" evolved from its premodern usage as "a noun of process: the tending of something, basically crops or animals" to three modern definitions:

> (i) the independent and abstract noun which describes a general
> process of intellectual, spiritual and aesthetic development, from C18
> [i.e., eighteenth century]; (ii) the independent noun, whether used
> generally or specifically, which indicates a particular way of life,
> whether of a people, a period or a group, from Herder and C19 . . . ;
> (iii) the independent and abstract noun which describes the works
> and practices of intellectual and especially artistic activity.[29]

As Williams indicates in (ii), this second modern usage of "culture," deriving from *Cultur* or *Kultur* in German, was initiated by the German philosopher Johann Herder. Williams explains:

> In his unfinished *Ideas on the Philosophy of the History of Mankind*
> (1784–91) [Herder] wrote of *Cultur*: "Nothing is more indeterminate
> than this word, and nothing more deceptive than its application to

27. Kathryne Lindberg, *Reading Pound Reading: Modernism after Nietzsche* (New York: Oxford University Press, 1987), 179.

28. See chapter 4 in this book.

29. Raymond Williams, *Keywords: A Vocabulary of Culture and Society* (New York: Oxford University Press, 1976), 80.

all nations and periods." . . . He argued, in a decisive innovation, *to speak of "cultures" in the plural: the specific and variable cultures of differ- ent nations and periods, but also the specific and variable cultures of social and economic groups within a nation. This sense, which has become common in 20C anthropology and sociology, and by extension in general use,* remained comparatively isolated, however, in all European lan- guages until at earliest mC19 and was not fully established until eC20. (79; emphasis added)

Williams goes on to identify that the German, Herderian definition of *Kultur,* "a particular way of life, whether of a people, a period or a group," was introduced into English by the founder of British anthro- pology, Edward Tylor, in his *Primitive Culture* (1870). This definition differs from that used by Matthew Arnold in *Culture and Anarchy* (1867), where "culture" refers to a process of "intellectual, spiritual and aes- thetic development"—the first of Williams's categories—or "the works and practices of intellectual and especially artistic activity"—the third of Williams's categories.

This important differentiation of the anthropological usage of the word from its English Arnoldian sense not only shows that Pound's cul- tural theory departs from, say, T. S. Eliot's Anglican elitism, but also identifies the Poundian theory's roots in modern anthropology. Pound declared that he had much to learn from Frobenius:

> The value of Leo Frobenius to civilization is not for the rightness or wrongness of this opinion or that opinion but for the kind of think- ing he does . . .
>
> He has in especial seen and marked out a kind of knowing, the difference between knowledge that has to be acquired by particular effort and knowing that is in people, "in the air." He has accented the value of such record. His archaeology is not retrospective, it is immediate. (*Guide* 57)

The Emersonian preference for a knowledge that is not "retrospective" but "immediate" is in close alliance with Pound's own ideology[30]—this, despite the difference, as Marjorie Perloff has pointed out, between Pound and Emerson in their views as to what constitutes a poem.[31] Just like Frobenius, Pound also had an anthropologist's zeal for collecting "data" from world cultures; and just like Frobenius, the Emersonian Pound assembled the data in order to document his theory of culture and to "immediately" reach into the "essence of culture," or *paideuma*. Commenting on *The Cantos*, Charles Bernstein trenchantly criticizes a panculturalism at work in Pound:

> Pound's great achievement was to create a work using ideological swatches from many social and historical sectors of his own society and an immense variety of other cultures. This complex, polyvocal textuality was the result of his search—his unrequited desire for— deeper truths than could be revealed by more monadically organized poems operating with a single voice and a single perspective.[32]

Imagism, which invented Chinese poetry and language by intertextual means, was one such folder containing "ideological swatches" from other cultures. An image, as defined by Pound, is "that which presents an intellectual and emotional complex in an instant of time" (*Literary* 4). In Imagism's invention of Chinese, an ethnographic *image* is also supposed to be presented immediately by applying the ideogrammic method or by means of the "direct treatment of the 'thing.'"

---

30. In the introduction to *Nature*, Ralph Waldo Emerson wrote, "Our age is retrospective. It builds the sepulchres of the fathers. It writes biographies, histories, and criticism. The foregoing generations beheld God and nature face to face; we, through their eyes" (*Essays* 7).

31. See Marjorie Perloff, *The Dance of the Intellect: Studies in the Poetry of the Pound Tradition* (Evanston, Ill.: Northwestern University Press, 1996). Perloff maintains that, for Poundians, it is meter rather than meter-making argument, as Emerson insists, that constitutes a poem. What I emphasize, however, is that so far as the conception of the "essence of culture" is concerned—essence embodied, for instance, by Chinese characters—Pound seems to stand in the Emersonian Transcendentalist tradition.

32. Charles Bernstein, *A Poetics* (Cambridge: Harvard University Press, 1992), 123.

Moreover, given our understanding of the usage of *Kulchur* by Pound, Chinese poetry became one of these cultures that represented to him a particular way of life, of a people or a group—a point that will become clearer in chapter 4 from a comparison of Imagism's representation of the Chinese language with the caricature made of Chinese in American pop culture. As Fenollosa stated without equivocation, "The study of Chinese poetry is an important part of the study of Chinese culture." In this sense Pound, whose ethnographic vision undergirded his poetry and poetics, came close to both Frobenius and Fenollosa. It was the commonality of an ethnographer's interest in *culture* that led Pound to pair Frobenius with Fenollosa when he wrote in an unpublished essay, "Understanding the Chinese Language": "Enlightened speculation would make use of Leo Frobenius *Childhood of Man* . . . [and] of Fenollosa's notes" (B83 F3623). Or when he wrote to Eliot in 1940:

> I know you jib at China and Frobenius cause they ain't pie church; and neither of us likes sabages, black habits, etc. However, for yr. enlightenment, Frazer worked largely from documents. Frob. went to *things*, memories still in the spoken tradition, etc. His students had to *see* and be able to draw objects. All of which follows up Fabre *and* the Fenollosa "Essay on Written Character." (*Selected Letters* 336)

What furthers the commonality between Frobenius and Fenollosa is the fact that Frobenius also collected African folktales in an effort to grasp the live speech of a tradition, or, as Pound put it, to "have gathered from the air a live tradition" (*Cantos* 522). In the same way, Fenollosa studied the Chinese poetry as a "fossil language" that had reserved "the best, the most hopeful and the most human elements" in Chinese culture.

Both *Kulchur* and *paideuma* lead to *Kulturmorphologie*, a term that was first used by Oswald Spengler and picked up by Frobenius and then by Pound. When culture is conceived of as a living organism, Guy Davenport writes, we can always "see through the debris of a civilization its paideumic structure which is never lost and which is ripe for rejuvenation and influence from the best of other cultures."[33] It is the alleged ability of culture to transform itself that has driven people "of no fortune but with a name to come" to embark upon a pilgrimage in search of the "live tradition in the air." But, as I have demonstrated, the desired immediacy of ethnographic truth cannot be achieved by means of the Imagistic "direct treatment of the 'thing'"; instead, it is contingent upon the intertextual relations in the world of intertexts. A live tradition, or a universal *Kulchur*, as Pound dreamt of, that transcends a particular way of a life and a people, cannot be gathered from the air but can only be reconstructed by intertextual means, such as retouching earlier translations, conflating texts, and even manufacturing examples. *Kulturmorphologie*, or the transformation of culture, is mediated by the transposition of intertexts.

Such intertextual transposition cannot simply be dismissed as "forgery," for what it reveals is a picture of incessant textual movements along the transpacific routes. From the Chinese legends to the Japanese interpretation, to Fenollosa's reinterpretation and re-creation, and to Pound's editing and his intertextual transposition that gave birth to his Imagistic poems was not a simple process of forgery, but a complex process of remaking culture. And it is a remaking that not only betrays Imagism as a modern ethnography of the Far East but also belies the intertextual nature of ethnography itself. Ethnography, to repeat my point, is what its etymology suggests: the writing of culture.

33. Guy Davenport, "Pound and Frobenius," in *Motives and Method in the Cantos of Ezra Pound*, ed. Lewis Leary (New York: Columbia University Press, 1954), 39.

THREE

The Intertextual Travel
of Amy Lowell

One "reads" a landscape the way one reads a text.
Michel de Certeau,
The Practice of Everyday Life

What follows is not a coda or supplement to Imagism, although Amy Lowell's work is often denigrated as such—"Amygism" is the usual epithet used to parody the poetry activities that went on after Lowell took over from Pound the leadership in promoting Imagism. My focus is on a new mode of conceptualizing Asia as manifested in Lowell's work. In the preceding chapter, I described the ways in which Pound founded his pancultural program on intertextual ground; in this one, I explore a unique feature of Lowell's ethnographic writing: her intertextual travel. As a traveler in the world of texts, the Imagist poet Lowell projected the *image* of the Far East in a manner characteristic of a tourist's fascination with a locale rather than an old-time ethnographer's devotion to a particular geographical area. However, Lowell's seemingly superficial intertextual travel should not be understood merely as following a shallow vogue of her time; but rather, it should be understood in the sense of what Michel de Certeau has termed "reading as poaching": "Readers are travelers; they move across lands belonging to someone else, like nomads poaching their way across fields they did not write, despoiling the wealth of Egypt to enjoy it themselves."[1] Moreover, I argue that intertextual travel is intrinsic to an ethnographic enterprise that uses texts as its fertile ground, its *field*, in an effort to generate ethnographic visions.

Amy Lowell (1874–1925) lived at a time, as she herself recognized, "of adulation of all things oriental."[2] It was the widespread craze of *japonisme* that took her elder brother Percival to the Far East. During the years he traveled in Japan and Korea, he wrote his little sister Amy many letters on Japanese decorated notepaper, which kindled her young imagination of the Wild East. As she later recalled,

> Every mail brought letters, and a constant stream of pictures, prints, and kakemonos flowed in upon me, and I suppose affected my imagination, for in childhood the imagination is plastic. . . . Japan seems entwined with my earliest memory. . . . [Those books and pictures] all through my childhood made Japan so vivid to my imagination that I cannot realize that I have never been there. (Qtd. in Damon, 55)

What this recollection reveals is not just the power of the imagination, but more important, the intertextual mode by which humans travel and see places they otherwise cannot see. It showcases what Paul Ricoeur has called "the world of the text." In his theories on hermeneutics Ricoeur made a radical move toward the concept of the textual world, one which we inhabit and wherein we project our ownmost possibilities. Ricoeur further characterizes such a world as follows:

> For me, the world is the ensemble of references opened up by every kind of text, descriptive or poetic, that I have read, understood, and loved. And to understand a text is to interpolate among the predi-

---

1. Michel de Certeau, *The Practice of Everyday Life*, trans. Steven Rendall (Berkeley and Los Angeles: University of California Press, 1984), 174.

2. Quoted in Foster Damon, *Amy Lowell: A Chronicle* (Hamden, Conn.: Archon Books, 1966), 329.

cates of our situation all the significations that make a *Welt* out of our *Umwelt*. It is this enlarging of our horizon of existence that permits us to speak of the references opened up by the texts or of the world opened up by the referential claims of most text.[3]

Like her fellow traveler Ezra Pound, Amy Lowell never set foot in the Far East; the land existed to her solely in textual terms. From the Japan in *Can Grande's Castle* (1918) to the China in *Pictures of the Floating World* (1919) and *Fir-Flower Tablets* (1921), the world of the Orient was one opened up by the kinds of texts she encountered and traversed: her brother's writings from and about Japan, her readings of Japanese and Chinese literatures, Ayscough's massive collection of "data" of Chinese poetry and culture, and her own Imagistic poems and translations of Chinese poetry. These texts seemed to have created for Lowell what Ricoeur calls an "as if" effect:

> Some texts . . . restructure for their readers the conditions of ostensive reference. Letters, travel reports, geographical descriptions, diaries, historical monographs, and in general all descriptive accounts of reality may provide the reader with an equivalent of ostensive reference in the mode of "as if" ("as if you were there"). (*Interpretation Theory* 35)

Such a verisimilitudinous effect may often be created, as Ricoeur remarks, by travelogues, a genre with which Lowell was intimately familiar.

Tourism to the Far East was on the steady rise during Amy Lowell's adult life, the early decades of the twentieth century. *Asia*, a magazine launched at the time to cater to the Oriental craze, was flooded by amateurish travel accounts, professional ethnographic studies, and travel agency advertisements. The booming business also attracted "serious" literati, among whom, for instance, was Eunice Tietjens, assistant editor of Harriet Monroe's *Poetry* (Chicago), a magazine that had played a key role in promoting Imagism. Tietjens was assigned by Monroe to go to

---

3. Paul Ricoeur, *Interpretation Theory: Discourse and the Surplus of Meaning* (Fort Worth: Texas Christian University Press, 1976), 37.

China and bring back accounts about the Oriental land. The result was the publication of Tietjens's *Profiles from China*—a collection of poems based on her trip—first in *Poetry* (1916) and then as a book (1917). For the book publication, Lowell wrote a review entitled "An Observer in China" in the September 1917 issue of *Poetry*. Lavishing her praise for Tietjens's poetic accomplishment, Lowell was also quick to notice the travelogue nature of these poems and the process in which the poetic traveler constructs the exotic, "half-apprehended" Other:

> *The Hand* is, not the orient (we could hardly expect that), but the occidental reaction to the orient; and what a happy inspiration it was to depict China under the guise of a hand: a large man with "the hand of a woman and the paw of a chimpanzee." The passage: "The long line of your curved nail is fastidiousness made flesh" *reveals the shrinking of the occidental mind in the face of the only half-apprehended East....*
>
> Mrs. Tietjens has lived in China, but she is not in the least of China. As interpretations of Chinese character, these poems are of only the slightest interest; it is as pictures of the fundamental antagonism of the East and the West that they are important. *The poet makes no pretence at an esoteric sympathy which she does not possess.* Her complete sincerity is not the least of the volume's excellences. Only in the section *Echoes* is there the slightest preoccupation with the native point of view ... still these poems remain rather as exercises in the Chinese manner, than as an intimate fusing of the author's ego with that of China.[4]

According to Lowell's review, "the author's ego" can never "fuse" with "that of China," since the East is only "half-apprehended" and the poet is seldom preoccupied with "the native point of view." Therefore, what's left is only the author's ego facing itself in the incomprehensible wilderness.

4. Amy Lowell, "An Observer in China," review of *Profiles from China*, by Eunice Tietjens, *Poetry* 10 (September 1917): 328–29; emphasis added.

Here a point Johannes Fabian has made about travel becomes relevant. In *Time and the Other: How Anthropology Makes Its Object*, Fabian analyzes the "topos of travel" utilized in the European Enlightenment:

> For the established bourgeoisie of the eighteenth century, travel was to become (at least potentially) every man's source of "philosophical," secular knowledge. Religious travel had been *to* the centers of religion, or *to* the souls to be saved; now, secular travel was *from* the centers of learning and power to places where man was to find nothing but himself.[5]

Fabian points out that the topos of travel as "a vehicle for self-realization of man" led to the secularization of Time for the eighteenth-century bourgeoisie and created a new discourse that was "based on an enormous literature of travelogues, collections and syntheses of travel accounts." And,

> [T]he manifest preoccupation in this literature, in its popular forms as well as in its scientific uses, was with the description of movements and relations in *space* ("geography") based primarily on visual observation of foreign *places*. (7)

Within the framework of Fabian's notion that the "topos of travel" is used as a vehicle for self-realization and that such a usage is often manifested in literature by the "visual observation of foreign places," I now examine the trajectories of Amy Lowell's intertextual travel and show how by "poaching" her way through the linguistic landscapes of the Far East, Lowell fashioned herself simultaneously as an Imagist poet and an intertextual traveler.

Lowell's closest contact with China came in her four years of collaboration with Ayscough on *Fir-Flower Tablets: Poems from the Chinese* (1921). Lowell explained the procedure of their collaboration as follows:

---

5. Johannes Fabian, *Time and the Other: How Anthropology Makes Its Object* (New York: Columbia University Press, 1983), 6.

Mrs. Ayscough would first write out the poem in Chinese. Not in the Chinese characters, of course, but in transliteration. Opposite every word she put the various meanings of it which accorded with its place in the text, since I could not use a Chinese dictionary. She also gave the analyses of whatever characters seemed to her to require it. (ix)

Lowell's part of work was to turn Ayscough's "literal translations into poems as near to the spirit of the originals as it was in my power to do" (v). Not knowing Chinese, Lowell had to depend on Ayscough (who depended on her Chinese teacher) as a travel guide who could take her through the textual landscape. Ayscough, who, as exemplified in *A Chinese Mirror*, had mastered the Chinese genre of literary tourism, turned out to be a very capable guide.[6] To facilitate Lowell's literary travel, she sent Lowell batches after batches of literal translations ("cribs"), as well as maps of Chinese landscapes and drawings of Chinese interior designs.

But the burden of the tour guide's work lay mainly in identifying the sensual scenery in the landscape of Chinese written characters. Let's take one poem to illustrate how Ayscough guided Lowell through the trip. The following is a poem by Tao Yuan-Ming (Pound's "To-Em-Mei"), entitled "Once More Fields and Gardens":

> Even as a young man
> I was out of tune with ordinary pleasures.
> It was my nature to love the rooted hills,
> The high hills which look upon the four edges of Heaven.
> What folly to spend one's life like a dropped leaf
> Snared under the dust of streets,
> But for thirteen years it was so I lived.
>
> The caged bird longs for the fluttering of high leaves.
> The fish in the garden pool languishes for *the whirled water*
> *Of meeting streams.*
> . . . .

---

6. See chapter 1 for my discussion of *A Chinese Mirror* as a travelogue modeled on the Chinese genre of literary tourism.

There is no dust or clatter
In the courtyard before my house.
My private rooms are quiet,
And calm with the leisure of moonlight through an open door.

(Fir 132–33; emphasis added)

Compared with the terseness of the five-character lines of Tao's original, Lowell's *vers libre* translation sounds more or less like a tourist's tedious journey.[7] But it is a journey that leads to the point where, facing the great scenery on the spot, one may experience the long-awaited moment of ecstasy. For the sake of such a revelatory experience, the lengthiness of boring transportation is truly worth the "trip."

The scenery spots in Chinese linguistic landscape through which Lowell traveled lay in places where a particular Chinese character was singled out, etymologically analyzed (by Ayscough, as a tour guide), and rendered into a phrase or a line in English. In the translation of Tao's poem, the phrase "the whirled water of meeting streams" stands for the Chinese character, 淵 (*yuan*, whirlpool). The line "And calm with the leisure of moonlight through an open door" also corresponds to just one character, 閑 (*xian*, leisure). What justified the seemingly disproportional rendition were, of course, the visual appearances of these characters. As Ayscough explains in "Amy Lowell and the Far East": "The pic-

---

7. A character-by-character literal translation of the corresponding lines from the poem runs like this:

young-no-fit-ordinary-tune
nature-originally-love-hills-mountains
mistakenly-fall-dust-net-midst
once-gone-three-ten-years
captive-birds-yearn-old-woods
pond-fish-miss-old-stream

. . . .

door-courtyard-no-dust-triviality
empty-room-has-extra-leisure

togram for 'a whirlpool' shows rivers which cross each other, and Miss Lowell's version reads: 'the whirled water of meeting streams.' "[8] The same with the character for "leisure," 閑, or 閒, which visually demonstrates "seeing the moon through the open door." Apart from these two places, the rest of the poem in Lowell's hand is a "literal," though at times loose and prosaic, rendition of the Chinese, in a manner Peter Boodberg has characterized as being "in favor of idiomatic clichés."[9] In contrast to Pound, who in his translations tried to intensify almost every line to make it sound more Imagistic and more "Oriental," Lowell seemed very concerned with particular characters, with those tourist spots in Chinese poetry that attract intertextual travelers like herself and Ayscough.

Recalling Fabian's notion that a Western tourist is usually preoccupied with visual observation of foreign places, we may be able to say here that these Chinese characters are those "foreign places" that Lowell, as an intertextual tourist, had chosen to observe visually: 淵, "the whirled water of meeting streams"; or, 閒, "the leisure of moonlight through an open door." Lowell chastised other translators who tried only to paraphrase the original in order to understand the culture: "It would be no good at all if you did it in free translation; no good at all as an approach to the Oriental mind, that is" (*Correspondence* 28). Just as Tietjens's travel poems reveal an obsession with the author/tourist's own experience in the foreign land, Lowell's translations create a travelogue, a narration of the translator/traveler's experience in the linguistic landscape that features such "hot spots" as 淵 and 閒. *Fir-Flower Tablets* highlights plenty of these revelatory moments, while rendering the rest of the poems almost "literally." It is no wonder that the Lowell / Ayscough collaboration has always been dismissed as an inferior comparison to the Pound / Fenollosa project, for critics often miss these

8. Florence Ayscough, *Florence Ayscough and Amy Lowell: Correspondence of a Friendship*, ed. Harley Farnsworth MacNair (Chicago: University of Chicago Press, 1945), 27.

9. See Peter Boodberg's comment on Ayscough in "Cedules from a Berkeley Workshop," now published in *Selected Works of Peter A. Boodberg*, comp. Alvin P. Cohen (Berkeley and Los Angeles: University of California Press, 1979), 182–83.

tourist "hot spots," unable to grasp a work that features above all the experience of intertextual travel.

Yet, devaluating a tourist's experience as "inauthentic" is a norm not only in literary studies; anthropology, for instance, from the very beginning has shared such a bias. Whereas realistic fiction (an oxymoron) has always been the preferred genre in literature when it comes to cultural description, social science–based ethnography has been regarded in anthropology as the only kind of work by means of which a culture can be adequately interpreted. The achievement of the authenticity requires vigorous fieldwork, which, in turn, entails physically *dwelling* among the Other. What therefore differentiates a professional ethnographer from a tourist is this fieldwork that fixes the former to the "field." However, such fixity, as James Clifford has argued, disguises the "travel" aspect of the anthropologist's work.[10] Or, to expand on Fabian, a social science–minded ethnographer travels to a remote village only to face his own ego, not in the wilderness, but in the midst of the scattered scientific, theoretic tools he has brought with him. To say that cultural knowledge thus procured may not always be different from strings of exotic beads or seashells a tourist takes home is not to dismiss all anthropological work as specious, but rather to foreground the intimate relationship between fieldwork and travel. Especially in the case of Amy Lowell, ethnographic representation of the Far East did take place in the field of language and text that she traversed.

■ ■ ■

> Forcing, abbreviating, pushing, padding, subtracting, riddling, interrogating, re-writing, she pulled text from text.
> *Susan Howe*, My Emily Dickinson

When Lowell asserted, as noted above, that poetry is "no good at all as an approach to the Oriental mind," she did not mean to deny the ethno-

10. See my earlier discussion of Clifford's *Routes: Travel and Translation in the Late Twentieth Century* (Cambridge: Harvard University Press, 1997) in chapters 1 and 2.

graphic function of poetry per se. Rather, she was dismissing the practice of interpreting poetry thematically in an effort to find ethnographic truth in it, a practice that went against the grain of her habit of reading. In his discussion of reading as poaching, Michel de Certeau distinguishes two acts involved in reading: one is the "lexical act" and the other the "scriptural act." Drawing upon results from psycho-linguistic experiments, de Certeau writes, "The schoolchild learns to read by a process that *parallels* his learning to decipher; learning to read is not a *result* of learning to decipher."[11] In other words, deciphering lexicons or comprehending meanings believed to be stored in texts constitutes only part of what we know as reading; the other part involves reading as a process comparable to that of inscribing: it entails wandering through a text, not observing the laws of ownership (meanings owned by untouchable texts), but rather inventing new relations between the text and the act of reading. To de Certeau, it is wrong to assume that to read is merely to receive a text from someone else without putting one's own mark on it, without remarking it. He believes that to read is to wander through an imposed system and to modify the text, that the reader "deterritorializes himself, oscillating in a nowhere between what he invents and what changes him," and that "to read is to be elsewhere . . . to constitute a secret scene, a place one can enter and leave when one wishes" (170–73). Looked at in this way, reading is not completely a hermeneutic act. Reading intends neither to reestablish nor to occupy the space of meaning promised by the text; instead, the reader moves through the textual space the way a traveler does through a landscape. And such a fascinating story about a reader's travel through texts— "drifts across the page, metamorphoses and anamorphoses of the text produced by the travelling eye, imaginary or meditative flights taking off from a few words, overlapping of spaces on the militarily organized surfaces of the text, and ephemeral dances"—remains, as de Certeau laments, in large measure untold (170). The remaining part of this chap-

11. Certeau, *Practice of Everyday Life*, 168.

ter, therefore, accompanies Lowell on her travels through texts, travels out of which came her poetic travelogues, produced in manners that Susan Howe has attributed to Lowell's New England predecessor, Emily Dickinson—that is, "she pulled text from text" by various means.[12]

In contrast to her fellow traveler Ezra Pound, who envisioned transcending cultural and linguistic boundaries, Lowell often foregrounded the differences between the East and West, as seen in her *Can Grande's Castle* (1918). This is a book of four long poems, or rather, four intertextual travelogues. The poetic vision moves from the Mediterranean in "Sea-Blue and Blood-Red" to Japan in "Guns As Keys: and the Great Gate Swings," to England in "Hedge Island," and finally back to the Mediterranean Sea in "The Bronze Horses." What makes this movement possible, as Lowell indicates in the preface, is her diligent digging into the dusty volumes of books:

> For it is obvious that I cannot have experienced what I have here
> written. I must have got it from books. But, living now, in the midst
> of events greater than these, the books have become reality to me in a
> way that they never could have become before, and the stories I have
> dug out of dusty volumes seem as actual as my own existence. (ix–x)

This daughter of New England did bow to her Transcendentalist forefathers who "beheld God and nature face to face," admitting that "this is the real decadence: to see through the eyes of dead men" (viii). But she immediately reassured herself of the necessity of seeing "through their eyes":

> Yet to-day can never be adequately expressed, largely because we are
> a part of it and only a part. For that reason one is flung backwards to
> a time which is not thrown out of proportion by any personal expe-
> rience, and which on that very account lies extended in something
> like its proper perspective. (viii)

12. Susan Howe, *My Emily Dickinson* (Berkeley: North Atlantic Books, 1985), 29.

The inadequacy of today and here creates a need for returning to yesterday and there not just transcendentally "on the viewless wings of Poesy" (Keats being Lowell's favorite poet, on whom she wrote a monograph), but more mundanely by digging into the books. Perhaps this is why Lowell not only chose Richard Aldington's poem "At the British Museum" as a motto to her book but also adopted Aldington's line as the title for her poetic travelogue:

> I turn the page and read . . .
> . . . .
> The heavy musty air, the black desks,
> The bent heads and the rustling noises
> In the great dome
> Vanish . . .
> And
> The sun hangs in the cobalt-blue sky . . .
> And the swallows dive and swirl and whistle
> About the cleft battlements of Can Grande's castle . . .

In this poem by Aldington, the reader is sitting inside the great dome built of books. He turns his eyes off the page for a moment and looks outside at the sunny blue sky and the battlements of the time-old castle; or is he looking through the page, through the words and eyes of the author he is reading, dead or alive?

The poetic traveler in Lowell's book is sightseeing through other books, however "decadent" it might seem to her New England forefathers. In "Guns as Keys," for instance, the postlude places in juxtaposition the Japan and the America of 1903, fifty years after Commodore Perry entered the Imperial gate of the East:

1903. JAPAN

The high cliffs of the Kegon waterfall, and a young man carving words on the trunk of a tree. He finishes, pauses an instant, and then leaps

into the foamcloud rising from below. But, on the tree-trunk, the
newly-cut words blaze white and hard as though set with diamonds:

"How mightily and steadily go Heaven and Earth! How infinite the
duration of Past and Present! Try to measure this vastness with five
feet. A word explains the Truth of the whole Universe—*unknowable.*
To cure my agony I have decided to die. Now, as I stand on the crest
of this rock, no uneasiness is left in me. For the first time I know that
extreme pessimism and extreme optimism are one."

1903. AMERICA

"Nocturne—Blue and Silver—Battersea Bridge.
Nocturne—Grey and Silver—Chelsea Embankment.
Variations in Violet and Green."
   Pictures in a glass-roofed gallery, and all day long the throng of
people is so great that one can scarcely see them. Debits—credits?
Flux and flow through a wide gateway. Occident—Orient—after
fifty years. (172–73)

But the first scene, a young Japanese jumping off the Kegon waterfall,
was witnessed and represented by Lowell only intertextually:

I owe the scene . . . to the paper "Young Japan," by Seichi Naruse,
which appeared in the "Seven Arts" for April, 1917. The inscription
on the tree I have copied word for word from Mr. Naruse's translation, and I wish here to express my thanks, not for his permission (as
with a perfect disregard of morals, I never asked it), but for his beautiful rendering of the original Japanese. I trust that my appreciation
will exonerate my theft. (xvi–xvii)

What Lowell humbly calls "theft" is often termed "quotation" in rhetoric. But as I argued earlier by way of Bakhtin and Kristeva, this intertextual strategy may also be called "transposition," a process of displacing
textual elements from one signifying system to another. Applied to
Lowell, transposition is an act of intertextual travel: she produces cul-

tural description by traveling through what Ricoeur has called "the ensemble of references opened up by the texts," and by means of what Susan Howe has described as "forcing, abbreviating, pushing, subtracting, riddling, interrogating, re-writing."[13]

As a whole, the poem "Guns as Keys" is a poetic narrative of the first encounter between the West and Japan in 1853. Part I unfolds the historical drama by staging a contrast on the level of composition: whereas the peaceful and aesthetic life of the Japanese is described in almost Imagistic lyrics, the aggressive, adventurous voyage of Commodore Perry's ship, the *Mississippi*, is written in the so-called polyphonic prose. These two styles alternate in the course of the poem's progression:

> At Mishima in the Province of Kai,
> Three men are trying to measure a pine tree
> By the length of their outstretched arms.
> Trying to span the bole of a huge pine tree
> By the spread of their lifted arms.
> Attempting to compress its girth
> Within the limit of their extended arms.
> Beyond, Fuji,
> Majestic, inevitable,
> Wreathed over by wisps of cloud.
> The clouds draw about the mountain,
> But there are gaps.
> The men reach about the pine tree,
> But their hands break apart;
> The rough bark escape their handclasps;
> The tree is unencircled.
> Three men are trying to measure the stem of a gigantic tree,
> With their arms,
> At Mishima in the Province of Kai. (163)

13. Ricoeur, *Interpretation Theory*, 36; Howe, *My Emily Dickinson*, 29.

The pastoral scene of a Sleepy Hollow–like legend, written in a simple, lyrical style, is immediately contrasted with a picture of the domineering, coal-burning, engine-running ship, depicted in polyphonic, prosaic words, mixtures of mechanical terminology and seafaring jargon:

> Furnaces are burning good Cumberland coal at the rate of twenty-six tons per diem, and the paddle-wheels turn round and round in an iris of spray. She noses her way through a wallowing sea; foots it, bit by bit, over the slanting wave slopes; pants along, thrust forward by her breathing furnaces, urged ahead by the wind draft flattening against her taut sails. (Ibid.)

The purpose for the contrast, Lowell explains, is that she "wanted to place in juxtaposition the delicacy and artistic clarity of Japan and the artistic ignorance and gallant self-confidence of America" (xvi). But in doing so, these "print-like lyrics," which "summarize Japanese civilization in its respective attitudes toward nature, sex, popular and aristocratic entertainments, the state, the church, the stage, politics, and death," have in effect ethnographically essentialized what is "Japanese."[14] For using what is supposed to be lyrics of "Oriental" style to represent the life of the Orient often works to the effect of reifying the Orientalist ideal, an effect experienced in Pound.

Yet, compared with Pound's transcendental view of a "world civilization," Lowell's essentialization at least recognizes the particularity of a culture: "the delicacy and artistic clarity of Japan" versus "the artistic ignorance and gallant self-confidence of America." Despite the differences, however, both Pound's pancultural *paideuma* and Lowell's relativist view of culture require certain authentication. Whereas Pound tried to collect "a live tradition in the air" by willfully misreading or mishandling textual samples, Lowell, who did not hide the fact that she was an intertextual traveler and that her writing of culture depended upon her readings, needed to authenticate by other means the knowledge thus acquired.

14. Damon, *Amy Lowell*, 474–75.

The authentication comes mainly in two ways, both of which are related to the scenes of "arrival" or gestures of "having-been-there" familiar in anthropological work. Since going to the field is defined in the discipline of anthropology as the stepping-stone for any ethnographic work, it is common for ethnographers either to begin with an account of their own arrival at the designated field or to devote at least some narrative passages to reassure of their "having been there" in the field.[15] However, for Lowell, who traveled in the intertextual world, her readerly arrival could not automatically validate the texts she traversed; the truth claims made in her writing would have to be confirmed by another physical arrival or having-been-there. Hence, first, in the case of translating Chinese poetry (or traveling through the landscape of Chinese poetry), she needed to establish the "authority" of her tour guide, Ayscough; and second, she bolstered her own travel account by soliciting positive responses from "reliable" readers and travelers.

On June 19, 1918, the eve of the first publication of her collaboration with Ayscough in *Poetry*, Lowell wrote to the editor Harriet Monroe:

> So I am afraid that you will have to take Mrs. Ayscough's and my final results as the best we can both of us do in the matter. She knows a lot about Chinese, and what passes her ear will, I am sure, satisfy you. You see she has had much more opportunity to know Chinese than most people, for she was born in China and lived there all her childhood, only coming home to finish her schooling and come out. She married when she was about twenty-two and returned to China, having also spent another Winter in China before that, bridging the time between her two residences there. She has lived there steadily now for twenty years, except for occasional visits to England and America. Chinese is, therefore, to some extent, her native tongue. For although she has only taken up the reading and speaking of it seri-

15. See also chapter 5 for another instance where the "arrival" trope is used in ethnographic writing.

ously in the last ten years, I think, she has been surrounded by the
sound of it, and the feel of it, and the psychology of it, all her life.[16]

A few days later, in a letter to Ayscough, Lowell wrote:

> I also gave her [Monroe] a great song and dance as to your
> qualifications as a translator. I told her that you were born in
> China, and that it was, therefore, in some sense your native tongue
> (Heaven forgive me!), although you had only taken up the serious
> study of it within the last few years. I lengthened out your years in
> China until it would appear that you must be a hundred years old to
> have got so many in, and altogether I explained that in getting you,
> she was getting the *ne plus ultra* of Chinese knowledge and under-
> standing; it being assumed, of course (though not by me expressed),
> that in getting me she was finding the best Englisher there was
> going. Anyhow, judging from the quick return upon herself evi-
> denced by this post card, she is properly impressed with what she
> will get, as a result. (Ibid. 38)

Establishing Ayscough's authority on the Chinese matter was crucial
because Lowell was, at the time, competing with Pound, who had published *Cathay* in 1915 and was trying to put out Fenollosa's article. Lowell lashed out at her competitor, as she wrote to Ayscough:

> My reason for suggesting that you put in the little hint of our
> discovery about roots is simply and solely to knock a hole in Ezra
> Pound's translations; he having got his things entirely from Pro-
> fessor Fenelosa *[sic]*, they were not Chinese in the first place, and
> Heaven knows how many hands they went through between the
> original Chinese and Professor Fenelosa's Japanese original.
> (Ibid. 43–44)

On another occasion, when Lowell wrote to the editor of the *Literary
Review*, which had published Arthur Waley's negative review of *Fir-*

---

16. Ayscough, *Correspondence*, 252.

Flower Tablets, she was again trying to get a lift not only from Ayscough but another "Chinese professor":

> Although I cannot read the Chinese characters, I have analysed a number of "fu" in transliteration with Mrs. Ayscough, and have lately talked the matter over at some length with a Chinese professor connected with one of our Universities, so I think I may make some claim to know whereof I speak. (Ibid. 259)

This "Chinese professor" turned out to be a Dr. Chao, about whom Lowell told Ayscough:

> I saw Dr. Chao last night, but it was a terrible disappointment. The child is a young boy, not long out of college, I should think, who is greatly interested in the new poetry movement in China, the writing of poetry in the vernacular, but has not kept up his classics at all.... Chao is a good little boy, but he is only teaching the Chinese language here, nothing to do with the literature; and, in spite of his compiling a new dictionary of rhymes, I do not think he has any literary sense. He told me before he came that he had only the knowledge of the classic literature which any educated non-literary Chinese would have, and that he was non-literary there was no manner of doubt when he arrived. (Ibid. 186–88)

No further commentary is necessary.

The second way to confirm the authenticity of the Japanese scenes she had intertextually created was by soliciting readers' responses to her poems. For instance, Lowell was always happy to tell this anecdote: After the appearance of "Guns As Keys" in a magazine, a Japanese wrote to her, "expressing his wondering admiration of [her] descriptive power," and, in closing, he even "asked how many years she had lived in his country!" (ibid. 21). Commenting on the lyrical poem starting with "At Mishima in the Province of Kai," which I quoted earlier, Ayscough wrote:

> Whoever has stood on the road above Mishima in the Province of Kai knows that this is a perfect description of the great Tokaido, the

Imperial highway lined with pine trees, which runs from Kyoto to Tokyo. (Ibid. 22)

A real tourist's "having-been-there" will confirm the intertextual tourist's recreation and will also confirm that

[T]he "tiger rain" of Japan falls just as Miss Lowell describes it in a later passage:

> Beating, snapping, on the cheese-rounds of open
> umbrellas,
> Licking, tiger-tongued, over the straw mat which
> a pilgrim wears upon his shoulders. (Ibid.)

An Imagistic scene. An Oriental(ist) scene. A traveler catches this snapshot of a pilgrim, another traveler, in the middle of a journey through the tiger-tongued raindrops (or words). But, isn't this a narcissistic reflection?

Lowell wrote in the first poem of her "Chinoiseries" in *Pictures of the Floating World:*

REFLECTIONS

When I looked into your eyes,
I saw a garden
With peonies, and tinkling pagodas,
And round-arched bridges
Over still lakes.
A woman sat beside the water
In a rain-blue, silken garment.
She reached through the water
To pluck the crimson peonies
Beneath the surface,
But as she grasped the stems,
They jarred and broke into white-green ripples;
And as she drew out her hand,
The water-drops dripping from it
Stained her rain-blue dress like tears. (27)

Whose eyes are these in which "I" sees the reflections of all these "essentially" Chinese things and the Chinese woman in the rain-blue silk dress? Maybe they are I's eyes? The crimson peonies beneath the surface of the water will be jarred and broken into white-green ripples when one tries to reach them; for they are only reflections of reality, of the real peonies. But soon as the water stills, they are there, again.

So it is the surface that creates, and hides.

So do words, in the world of intertexts.

FOUR

The Multifarious Faces of the Chinese Language

In the "search for oneself," in the search for "sincere self-expression," one gropes, one finds some seeming verity. One says "I am" this, that, or the other, and with the words scarcely uttered one ceases to be that thing.

Ezra Pound, "Vorticism"

> I posed
> as a cookie
> fortune smeller
>
> *John Yau,*
> *"Genghis Chan:*
> *Private Eye XX"*

Imagism has created an "image" of Oriental cultures projected in language. Whether in Pound's giant pancultural program or in Lowell's intertextual travel narrative, an Orientalist "image," in the form of both poetic effect and cultural description, stands out conspicuously, like "petals on a wet, black bough." This double meaning of "image" thus bespeaks the twin projects that the Imagist Pound and Lowell were pursuing: on the one hand they were creating a modernist poetry, and on the other hand they were writing ethnographies of the Far East and looking at culture from a particular standpoint. And these two projects, as I have tried to show, cannot be discussed in isolation; instead, Imagism's symbiosis resonates with what James Clifford has called the "predicament" of the twentieth century—"a pervasive condition of off-centeredness in a world of distinct meaning systems, a state of being in culture while looking at culture."[1] In a poetic ethnography such as Imagism, culture ceases to be a preexisting entity; it becomes emergent from ethnographic writing. Consequently, cultural meanings, losing their distinctness, articulate themselves only in forms of migration and displacement.

Let us imagine: Charlie Chan (a fictional Chinese American detective from Honolulu) meets up with Ezra Pound (an elite poet from Philadelphia) at an obscure limehouse tea shop. After the initial greetings, which are delivered in the most proper manner, the subject of their conversation comes naturally to one that concerns both of them deeply: the Chinese language. Only a few minutes into the topic, there seems to arise some sort of disagreement. The poet, apparently out of frustration, dips his right index finger into his tea bowl, draws out some tea water, and scribbles on the dark, smooth surface of the table. Where the trace of water stretches and shrinks, there appears a Chinese character, 信 (*xin*). Paraphrasing Confucius, the poet explains the meaning of the character, which happens to be one of his favorites: "Man stands by his word."[2] In response, the master detective dishes out a pidgin version of a good old Confucian witticism, as he often does in the novels and films: "Tongue often hang man quicker than rope." In like manner the gentlemen's brain wrestling continues . . .

1. James Clifford, *The Predicament of Culture: Twentieth-Century Ethnography, Literature, and Art* (Cambridge: Harvard University Press, 1988), 9.

2. *Xin* is also the first Chinese character to have appeared in Pound's cantos (vide Canto XXXIV). In "Some Notes by a Very Ignorant Man," a supplement to the 1935 publication of Ernest Fenollosa's *The Chinese Written Character as a Medium for Poetry*, Pound interprets this character as "Man and word, man standing by his word, man of his word, truth, sincere, unwavering" (47).

This imaginary scene, despite its apparent absurdity, helps to illustrate a simple but significant fact: American pop culture's creation of a demeaning image of the Orient—as in the case of Charlie Chan—was strikingly contemporaneous with modern American poetry's cultivation of a genuine interest in Oriental languages—as in the case of Imagism. In the preceding chapters, I have described this interest as simultaneously poetic and ethnographic. In this transitional chapter, I continue to investigate Imagism's ethnographic enterprise, but in a different context. The "image" created by Imagism is but one of the many faces twentieth-century America has drawn for the Chinese language. Imagism's linguistic mimicry should, I submit, be understood in the context of American pop culture's pidginization of Chinese, and both the mimicry and pidginization will be subject to countermocking in the work of Asian writers and Asian American writers such as Lin Yutang and John Yau. In all these instances, whether the writer means to idealize or demean, to mock or countermock, linguistic mimesis in its various formations remains a powerful tool of cultural description.

■　■　■

> "The secret is to talk much, but say nothing."
> *Charlie Chan in Earl Derr Biggers,*
> Keeper of the Keys *(1932)*

The genesis of Charlie Chan is a modern legend: one day, Earl Derr Biggers, author of the successful mystery novel *Seven Keys to Baldpate*, was basking in the sunlight of Honolulu when he came upon a report in a local newspaper about a Chinese detective named Chang Apana. Biggers had never heard of an Oriental detective, although he was, like everybody else at that time, familiar with Dr. Fu Manchu. A novel idea dawned upon him, and he started a new book called *The House without a Key* (1925), in which an Oriental detective from Honolulu, Charlie Chan, made his debut. The book was an instant success, and Biggers produced, before his death in 1933, five more Charlie Chan novels, all of which, with one exception, were made into movies that still run today.

In both the novels and the movies, one of the objects of laughter is of course Charlie's stocky body. But what is more fascinating and ensures the character's popularity is the manner in which he speaks. Unlike Sherlock Holmes, who puffs and muses, Charlie is characteristically voluble. As he himself admits, "Talk is my weakness."[3] He speaks Mandarin Chinese, Cantonese, English, Hawaiian, French, and who knows what else. His adroitness in shifting these linguistic gears is a big plus in his success as a detective. At times a short conversation with his Chinese informant, which sounds like only singsong and is therefore completely incomprehensible to the Anglo-Americans on the spot, can lead him to the essential clue to the murder case at hand. But nothing can compare with his mouthful, or stomachful, of half-baked fortune-cookie Confucian aphorisms, which he can dish out as the occasion demands. Let me provide a short list:

Always harder to keep secret than for egg to bounce on sidewalk.
Way to find rabbit's residence is to turn rabbit loose and watch.
Some heads, like hard nuts, much better if cracked.
Too late to dig well after honorable house is on fire.
Mind like parachute—only function when open.
Events explode suddenly like fire crackers in the face of innocent
    passerby.

What characterizes these witticisms is not the wisdom one can find in a wise man's saying such as Benjamin Franklin's "God helps those that help themselves." Charlie's proverbs are pidginized—the sentences lack subjects, the nouns lack articles, the verbs are not conjugated—and intended not to enlighten, but to baffle. In *Black Camel* (1929), for example, Charlie confronts a murder suspect by pulling out a spicy item from his proverbial stock:

Jaynes pushed forward. "I have important business on the mainland,
    and I intend to sail at midnight. It is now long past ten. I warn you that

---

3. Earl Derr Biggers, *Keeper of the Keys* (1932; reprint, New York: Bantam Books, 1975), 177.

you must call out your entire force if you propose to keep me here—"

"That also can be done," answered Charlie amiably.

"Good lord!" The Britisher looked helplessly at Wilkie Ballou. "What kind of place is this? Why don't they send a white man out here?"

A rare light flared suddenly in Charlie's eyes. "The man who is about to cross a stream should not revile the crocodile's mother," he said in icy tones.

"What do you mean by that?" Jaynes asked. (104–5)

Charlie knows very well the effectiveness of his talk, which is only half-comprehensible to most of his listeners. He enjoys getting people to ask, as Jaynes did, "What do you mean by that?" or "What does it mean in English?" although he *is* speaking English, if pidginized English. The psychological advantage he gains by baffling people is one of his hidden weapons in the sleuthing business. "The secret," as he tells a white colleague who is not good at talking, "is to talk much, but say nothing" (*Keeper* 137). But this talk-much-but-say-nothing business sometimes gets Charlie into trouble, especially when clear speech is needed. He is once publicly humiliated when appearing in court as the key witness:

"I am walking down Pawaa Alley," he [Charlie] remarked. "With me is my fellow detective, Mr. Kashimo. Before us, at the door of Timo's fish shop, we perceive extensive crowd has gathered. We accelerate our speed. As we approach, crowd melts gradually away, and next moment we come upon these three men, now prisoners in the dock. They are bent on to knees, and they disport themselves with dice. Endearing remarks toward these same dice issue from their lips in three languages."

"Come, come, Charlie," said the prosecuting attorney, a red-haired, aggressive man. "I beg your pardon—Inspector Chan. Your language is, as usual, a little flowery for an American court. These men were shooting craps. That's what you mean to say, isn't it?"

"I am very much afraid it is," Chan replied. (*Charlie Chan* 133)

Partly because of the unsuitableness of Charlie's florid diction in court, and partly because Kashimo, his Japanese sidekick, lost the dice they had confiscated as evidence, the charge is dismissed and the three crap-shooters walk out free, much to Charlie's dismay. Hence the floweriness of his speech, which at times aids him, can become Charlie's stumbling block.

Charlie Chan and his nuggets of fortune-cookie Confucius will provide a good laugh only if we don't realize that they were all created by Biggers. It should be evident that this creation epitomizes a racist conception of the Chinese language and its speakers, for Charlie's metaphoric diction sounds all too familiar to readers of modern racist literature that depicts mysterious, inscrutable Orientals with their expressionless faces and slanting eyes. In this respect, Charlie's flowery and slippery speech resonates with the poisonous devil's tongue of Dr. Fu Manchu, an Oriental protagonist created by Sax Rohmer in an earlier series of equally popular detective stories. Under Rohmer's pen, Fu Manchu, a modern Satan from the East who designs an evil plot to take over the West, speaks in florid metaphors, as does Charlie Chan. What these two creations helped to fashion and substantiate in the early decades of this century was a stereotype of the racial Other's language and, more important, a stigmatization of the race.

Imagism appears to entail a very different conception of the same language. Two of the three principles put down by Pound in "A Few Don'ts by an Imagiste" stress directness and clarity in poetic diction: "1. Direct treatment of the 'thing' whether subjective or objective. 2. To use absolutely no word that does not contribute to the presentation" (*Literary* 3). And as I have argued, Imagism's aesthetic principle is closely tied to its encounter with the Chinese language from an ethnographic standpoint. What especially attracted the Imagists was what Fenollosa saw as its "naturalness," or what Jespersen called its "modernity." The naturalness, according to Fenollosa, is defined by, among other things, the clarity with which the language demonstrates, in its grammatical structure and in individual words, the transference of force from the agent to the object in the same manner that it takes place in nature (*CWC* 16). Compared with the floridity and nonsense attributed to Chinese in racist literature like the Charlie Chan series, Imagism's characterization of that language obviously ran the opposite course.

Identifying this incongruity between two contemporary conceptions of the Other's language has at least two corollaries. First, it becomes evident once again that just as the racist portrayal of the Orient in American pop culture was thoroughly ethnographic, Imagism's description of the language was equally so from the same perspective. Second, this incongruity testifies in part to the inadequacy of a kind of reductive contextualization that can be found in recent studies of "nativist" modernism. Walter Benn Michaels, for instance, asserts in his revisionist project *Our America: Nativism, Pluralism and Modernism* (1995) that American modernism is inextricably connected to American nativism. He makes a connection between what he calls modernism's "identitarianism" and the racist discourse of the same period, maintaining that modernist poetic terms are indistinguishable from the 1920s terms of racial identity, and that the promulgation of racial identity is made literally indistinguishable from strategies of literary narration. The stark contrast between Imagism and its contemporary racist literature in terms of how they project the image of the Orient belies this assertion.[4] However, to use Imagism's somewhat benign view, versus the racist view, of the racial Other's language as an example to undermine Michaels's argument is hardly my point here, because there is a far more important issue at stake. The weakness of Michaels's project lies not so much in his denigration of modernism as in his not grasping the significance of modernism's linguistic encounter with the Other.

Writing in a different context, Stephen Greenblatt identifies similar variations in attitude that one culture holds toward the language of the Other—in his case, the Old World's view of Native American speech.

---

4. One may also, as Marjorie Perloff points out, think of many canonical modernist writers such as Ezra Pound, T. S. Eliot, H. D., Gertrude Stein, Djuna Barnes, and Wallace Stevens, who may not fit into Michaels's nativist paradigm (Perloff, "Modernism without the Modernists: A Response to Walter Benn Michaels," *MODERNISM/Modernity* 3.1 [1996]: 100).

Greenblatt emphasizes two European beliefs that he finds to be equally colonialist: one was that Indian language was deficient or nonexistent and the other was that there was no serious language barrier between Europeans and savages.[5] The first view apparently corresponds to that presented in the Charlie Chan series, which deems the Oriental languages to be defective and inscrutable. The second, albeit not completely applicable to Imagism, may shed some light on our understanding of the radical ways American modernism has put to use its linguistic experience with the Other. Greenblatt suggests that the historical and philosophical reasons for the denial of the language barrier between the Old and New Worlds lie in that "embedded in the narrative convention [of the sixteenth century] was a powerful, unspoken belief in the isomorphic relationship between language and reality," a belief that in the seventeenth century grew into a search for a universal language (28). As I mentioned earlier, this idea of a universal language found its way into nineteenth-century Transcendentalist philosophy, which, in turn, bore strongly on the work of Fenollosa, Pound, and A. Lowell. Yet the cachet of Imagism lies not just in identifying Chinese as a paragon of the universal language, but more important in appropriating foreign linguistic signs into its own signifying practice. And in doing so, Imagism pushed the Western language project a step further while opening up a transnational route for "American" literature.

■ ■ ■

> Now don't you think my makeup's good?
> The man who fixed me said he thought
> I'd done it all my life. You should
> Have seen me put it on—I bought
> It down in the pawnshop row.
> I think we'll have a dandy show.
>
> *Sidney Toler, "Stage Fright"*

5. Stephen Greenblatt, *Learning to Curse: Essays in Early Modern Culture* (New York: Routledge, 1990), 16–39.

When Sidney Toler wrote this title poem of his book of poetry (published in 1910), he could not have envisioned that his "makeup" would really be thought "good" two decades later by many who were enraptured by his "yellowface" performances as Charlie Chan on the silver screen. Indeed, in all the films made and remade from the early 1930s to the late 1940s, the role of Charlie was always played by white actors: Warner Oland, Sidney Toler, and Roland Winters. Whereas Toler needed a mask in order to look Asian, Oland, because of the mixed blood he inherited from Swedish and Russian parents, looked naturally Chinese.

In the novels, the racial masquerade is even more twisted. Not only does the author Biggers hide behind the puppet show, cooking his Confucius in Charlie's mouth, but also Charlie himself often puts on a mask. In *The Chinese Parrot* (1926), for instance, Charlie has to disguise himself as a Chinese servant named Ah Kim in order to stake out a rich man's house and solve the mystery. Although Charlie's English is already a flowery pidgin, as Ah Kim he has to speak in a still less standard manner, saying such things as "allight, boss." It is not a happy situation for him, as he complains: "All my life...I study to speak fine English words. Now I must strangle all such in my throat, lest suspicion rouse up" (70). But on other occasions he enjoys using the masquerade to trick others, the same way he uses metaphoric talk to baffle people. Here is an example from the same novel:

> "But listen, Charlie," Eden protested. "I promised to call my father
> this morning. And Madden isn't an easy man to handle."
> "Hoo malimali," responded Chan.
> "No doubt you're right," Eden said. "But I don't understand
> Chinese."
> "You have made natural error," Chan answered. "Pardon me while
> I correct you. That are not Chinese. It are Hawaiian talk. Well known
> in islands—hoo malimali—make Madden feel good by a little harmless
> deception. As my cousin Willie Chan, captain of All-Chinese baseball
> team, translate with his vulgarity, kid him along." (78)

This is a case of double masquerading: the author masquerades as Charlie, who masquerades as a (speaker of) Chinese. Charlie's purpose in
saying something in Hawaiian as if it were Chinese is to warn his lis-
tener not to make a natural error, such as presuming that he can be
nothing but Chinese. In fact, Charlie is very ambiguous about his Chineseness. In *Keeper of the Keys*, comparing himself to Ah Sing—an old
servant who has kept his Chineseness intact—Charlie says:

> "It overwhelms me with sadness to admit it . . . for he is of my own
> origin, my own race, as you know. But when I look into his eyes I
> discover that a gulf like the heaving Pacific lies between us. Why?
> Because he, though among Caucasians many more years than I, still
> remains Chinese. As Chinese to-day as in the first moon of his exis-
> tence. While I—I bear the brand—the label—Americanized. . . . I
> traveled with the current. . . . I was ambitious. I sought success. For
> what I have won, I paid the price. Am I an American? No. Am I,
> then, a Chinese? Not in the eyes of Ah Sing." (87)

Here, Charlie's confession sounds like an evangelical sermon on cultural
assimilationism, a white man's sermon delivered through a masquerading yellow man's lips. Moreover, the stigmatized yellow man is pushed
to confront the question of racial identity. But even as he is made to
lament the loss of imagined pure Chineseness, his flowery, pidginized,
and ultimately defective speech has already doubly bound him to a racial
stigma. As a white police sergeant tells him: "You're all right. Just like
chop suey—a mystery, but a swell dish."[6]

Undoubtedly, Charlie Chan is an emblem of racial parody and his
speech a pidginization of Chinese. In contrast, Imagism seems able to
sever linguistic traits from a stereotyped racial identity, performing ventriloquism without parody. Here are some Imagistic poems in which
ventriloquism is obviously at work. The first one, entitled "From
China" (1919) is by Amy Lowell:

6. Quoted in Ken Hanke's *Charlie Chan at the Movies: History, Filmography and Criticism* (Jefferson, N.C.: Mcfarland, 1989), 88.

FROM CHINA

I thought:—
The moon,
Shining upon the many steps of the palace before me,
Shines also upon the chequered rice-fields
Of my native land.
And my tears fell
Like white rice grains
At my feet.

(Complete Works 204)

Here, the New England noblewoman sits in her Sevenel Mansion in Brookline, Massachusetts, and speaks through the mouth of a Chinese concubine from the countryside. With the moon and such phrases as "steps of the palace," "rice-fields," and "rice grains" embodying an evident literary Orientalism, the ventriloquism achieves its poetic effect without parodying the character. The same with another poem by Lowell, entitled "Near Kyoto" (1919):

NEAR KYOTO

As I crossed over the bridge of Ariwarano Narikira
I saw that the waters were purple
With the floating leaves of maples

(Ibid. 203)

What is being masqueraded here is a Japanese voice, one that even pronounces an untranslated Japanese name: Ariwarano Narikira. But again, the imagined "crossing over" of the racial "bridge" is not focused on the racial identity itself; instead, it only attempts to capture the somewhat clichéd motifs of Oriental poetry: bridge, water, floating leaves, maples.

In matters of linguistic mimicry, Pound is a master. He first tried his hand in Chinese ventriloquism in the four poems collected in the 1914 Imagist anthology: "After Ch'u Yuan," "Liu Ch'e," "Fan-Piece for Her

Imperial Lord," and "Ts'ai Chi'h." They are often read as creative translation but should also be read as linguistic mimicry, as in "After Ch'u Yuan":

> I will get me to the wood
> Where the gods walk garlanded in wisteria,
> By the silver blue flood move others with ivory cars.
> There come forth many maidens
>   to gather grapes for the leopards, my friend,
> For there are leopards drawing the cars.
>
> I will walk in the glade,
> I will come out from the new thicket
>   and accost the procession of maidens (43)

The poetic persona assumes the voice of the first Chinese poet, Ch'u Yuan, and walks with it—in today's parlance, He walks the walk and talks the talk. The odd, archaic sentence structure of "I will get me to the wood" corresponds to a scene exoticized with phrases such as "garlanded in wisteria," "silver blue flood," "ivory cars," "gather grapes for the leopards," "leopards drawing cars," and so on.

Pound's *Cathay* (1915), which re-creates Chinese poetic motifs through translation, is the culmination of his Chinese ventriloquism, so much so that Eliot even called him "the inventor of Chinese poetry" ("Introduction" xvi). In "The Jewel Stairs' Grievance," for example, Pound identifies himself with the poetic voice of Li Po (Rihaku), who in turn identifies with the female "I" in the poem:

> The jewelled steps are already quite white with dew,
> It is so late that the dew soaks my gauze stockings,
> And I let down the crystal curtain
> And watch the moon through the clear autumn. (13)

It should be evident that the poetic "identification" here is by no means "identitarian," a feature Michaels claims to be crucial to modernism (*Our America* 141). For this is not a *racialized* masquerade; nor is the "transcreation" of features of the Chinese language intended as a mocking of its speakers. Instead, what lies at the heart of Pound's *Cathay*, of Imagism as a whole, is an effort to find a different "medium for poetry," as indicated clearly in the title of Fenollosa's essay—"The Chinese Written Character as a Medium for Poetry."

To say that race is not a crucial factor in the Imagists' ventriloquism is not to suggest simply that the Imagists were not racists, but rather to emphasize that their interest in linguistic traits has not led them to stereotype the racial identity that is often, as in popular racist literature, associated with a language. In *The Dialect of Modernism: Race, Language, and Twentieth-Century Literature*, Michael North argues that the mimicry of black vernacular provides white modernists with a "technical distinction" and "insurrectionary opposition" to linguistic standardization in English. He writes,

> In fact, three of the accepted landmarks of literary modernism in English depend on racial ventriloquism of this kind: Conrad's *Nigger of the "Narcissus,"* Stein's "Melanctha," and Eliot's *Waste Land*. If the racial status of these works is taken at all seriously, it seems that linguistic mimicry and racial masquerade were not just shallow fads but strategies without which modernism could not have arisen.[7]

What North conceives as essential to modernism—the mimicry of black vernacular—is to a large extent analogous to Imagism's Chinese ventriloquism. And the analogy is even borne out by Pound's use of black dialect in his translation of Confucian Odes, as in this one:

> Yalla' bird, you stay outa dem oaks,
> Yalla' bird, let them crawps alone,
> I just can't live with these here folks,

7. Michael North, *The Dialect of Modernism: Race, Language, and Twentieth-Century Literature* (New York: Oxford University Press, 1994), v.

> I gotta go home and I want to git goin'
> To whaar my dad's folks still is a-growin'.
>
> *(Classic Anthology* 100)

Or in this ode where the translator / ventriloquist Pound adopts "the oldest cliché of the dialect tradition, the black freedman's nostalgia for the plantation" (North 99):

> Don't chop that pear tree,
> Don't spoil that shade;
>
> Thaar 's where ole Marse Shao used to sit,
> Lord, how I wish he was judgin' yet.
>
> *(Classic Anthology* 8)

It should be obvious that what Michaels has called "identity essentialism" may not be a very accurate characterization of American modernism when it comes to the issue of language. The nativist approach that thematizes a period of literature as a search for racial identity often underestimates the slipperiness of cross-cultural appropriations and fails to identify signifying mechanisms in literary texts that stand on racial and linguistic boundaries. The pidginization of Chinese in Charlie Chan is indeed a racist stereotyping, but the poetic ventriloquism of Imagism constitutes an example of cultural translation, by which "foreign" systems of meaning are appropriated so as to develop new ways of signification in the "home" culture.

∎ ∎ ∎

> I think pidgin a glorious language. It has tremendous possibilities.
>
> *Lin Yutang, "In Defense of Pidgin English"*

Whether looked at as the ideal Adamic language or as the poisonous Devil's tongue, Chinese continues to fascinate twentieth-century America, and the representations of it remain varied. Whereas the Chinese as a race, according to Robert G. Lee in *Orientals: Asian Americans in Popular Culture* (1999), has at least six faces in American racist or racialist representations—the pollutant, the coolie, the deviant, the yellow peril, the model minority, and the gook—the Chinese language is also portrayed in multifarious images. What is in Imagism and Charlie Chan are but two extreme representations, both of which will compete with a throng of others and be subject to revision by them. Especially notable is the meticulous reconstruction of the "new" image of Chinese in the hands of Chinese American writers, whose work often absorbs the clichés about the language, but revises them and subjects them to double parody or countermockery. Two writers are examples: one is the midcentury essayist Lin Yutang, and the other is the contemporary poet John Yau.

Lin Yutang (1895–1976) had been an important modern Chinese writer before he moved to the United States in 1936 and became an author of best-selling books in English about China. His *My Country and My People* (1935), in particular, was an instant success and was reprinted twelve times within three years. Lin[8] was well known for his prose style, one that can be best characterized as full of gentle humor or irony. But such idiosyncrasy in his writing is often misunderstood as "whitewashing." Xiao-huang Yin, for instance, remarks in his otherwise very important essay, "Worlds of Difference" (1998), "Lin Yutang's English writing seems 'whitewashed' to collaborate in rather than challenge the stereotyping images of the Chinese in the West." And what makes Yin come to such a conclusion is the "polite and self-mocking tone, light-hearted jokes, and apolitical attitude" that characterize Lin's English writing.[9] Elaine Kim, in *Asian American Literature* (1982), goes

8. "Lin" is Lin Yutang's last name. He did not follow the common practice of reversing the order of surname and given name when Chinese names are transliterated into English.

9. Xiao-huang Yin, "Worlds of Difference: Lin Yutang, Lao She, and the Significance of Chinese-Language Writing in America," in *Multilingual America: Transnationalism, Ethnicity, and the Languages of American Literature*, ed. Werner Sollors (New York: New York University Press, 1998), 180.

even further in condemning Lin's seeming lightheartedness: "Lin's writing is in the main amiable nonsense, passing for 'Chinese' or 'philosophy.' His heavy-handed aphorisms are almost parodies, *lacking even the wit of the fictional Charlie Chan.*"[10]

These critics' misunderstanding of Lin's work seems to have originated in their inability to come to terms with his profound critique of the West, which is often couched in his apparent self-mockery as a Chinese. One aspect of the seriousness of his critique can be found in his mockery of the so-called Basic English and his advocacy of Pidgin English. In the context that Chinese was being regarded in modern America either as an ideal language or as a debased tongue, Lin promoted a hybrid of English and Chinese, "Chinglish," that cuts both ways. He responded critically to the efforts of purification made by some linguists to facilitate the adoption of English as a medium of international intercourse. He targeted especially the program of Basic English, started by C. K. Ogden. Ogden's idea was to limit the basic English vocabulary to eight hundred and fifty words, which are supposed to cover all the bare needs of communication in English. Of these eight hundred and fifty, the first hundred consist of "operators," including eighteen verbs (*come, get, give, go, keep, let, make, put, seem, take, be, do, have, say, see, send, may,* and *will*) and words like *if, because, so, as, just, only, but, to, for, through, yes,* and *no*. There are four hundred "general names" like *copper, cork, copy, cook,* and *cotton;* two hundred "common things" or "picturables" like *cake, camera, card, cart,* and *cat;* and one hundred and fifty "qualifiers," or adjectives, like *common, complex,* and *conscious.*[11] This is no doubt a highly purified list of English words, making no room for any hybridization or borrowing from the vocabulary of nonnative speakers, as was constantly taking place in everyday English when Lin was writing. One consequence of this principle of purification, Lin points out, is falling into utter circumlocution:

10. Elaine Kim, *Asian American Literature: An Introduction to the Writings and Their Social Context* (Philadelphia: Temple University Press, 1982), 28; emphasis added.

11. Lin Yutang, *The Little Critic: Essays, Satires and Sketches on China,* 2d series, 1933–35 (Westport, Conn.: Hyperion Press, 1935), 49.

"The most fervent image of imagination" becomes "the most burning picture that has existence only in mind"; a "beard" becomes "growth of hair on the face"; and a woman's "breast" becomes a "milk-vessel" (*Little Critic* 52–53). He quotes a passage from a story titled "Carl and Anna" as rewritten in Basic English:

> Slowly he went to her, feeling her attraction. There was something troubled about her parted lips; at the same time they said "yes." He put his arm slowly round her. They were together in one another's arms, not moving. And when, lifting his eyes, he saw her lips open, waiting for him, and *took them again and again*, no word was said. (53)

One may find such an extremely circumlocutious passage nowhere else except in the work of another self-labeled linguistic purist—Henry James. The reason I mention James here is not, however, his idiosyncratic circumlocution but rather his notion about the purity of the English language, which provides another backdrop for our understanding of Lin's promotion of Pidgin English. In his 1905 lecture to the graduates at Bryn Mawr College, which is entitled *The Question of Our Speech*, James chastised the immigrant population—the Dutch, the Irish, the Italian, etc.—for "playing, to their heart's content, with the English language, or in other words, dump[ing] their mountain of promiscuous material into the foundations of the American."[12] Although not specified by James as the linguistic pollutants (probably because they belonged to an even lower linguistic status), the Chinese were certainly among the people who had made English into what he called "an easy and ignoble minimum" barely distinguishable from "the grunting, the squealing, the barking, or the roaring of animals" (16). Interestingly, James also blamed American modernist writers for accelerating the fragmentation of culture by their adoption of "nonstandard" speeches in their work, a practice that was to be continued by the Imagists only a few years later.

---

12. Henry James, *The Question of Our Speech* (Boston: Houghton Mifflin, 1905), 42–43.

In his speech, James was by no means advocating the kind of Basic English that reduces the function of English to mere communication without claims to literary beauty. However, it is evident that James shared with other linguistic purists an aversion to the hybridization of language, an aversion that would become the object of Lin's critique in his prose essays. It is worth noting that Lin had always been interested in the issue of linguistic hybridity. He studied comparative literature at Harvard between 1919 and 1920 and then went to Germany to work on his master's thesis on the evolution of the spoken language, particularly the development of Chinese dialects as a result of race mixture, colonization, and migration. At the peak of his literary career—that is, in the 1930s, he wrote a number of essays on the issue of English and Chinese, advocating Chinglish. In the essay entitled "In Defense of Pidgin English" (circa 1934), Lin unleashes an ironist's humor, or a humorist's irony, in mocking the opponents of pidgin. He begins the essay by stating that

> I think pidgin a glorious language. It has tremendous possibilities.
> So far as I know, Bernard Shaw and Otto Jespersen are the only
> people who have a good word to say for pidgin. In a newspaper
> interview, Shaw is quoted as saying that the pidgin "no can" is a
> more expressive and more forceful expression than the "unable" of
> standard English. When a lady says she is "unable" to come, you
> have a suspicion she may change her mind and perhaps come after
> all, but when she replies to your request with an abrupt, clear-cut
> "no can," you know you have to reckon without her company.[13]

Being expressive is only one of pidgin's advantages over standard English. In a tone of what Elaine Kim has dismissed as "amiable nonsense," Lin continues to account for the bright future of pidgin:

> Even the historical dialect of Karl Marx makes it inevitable that pidgin English shall become the language spoken by all the respectable people of the world in the twenty-fifth century. Advocates of English

---

13. Lin Yutang, *The Little Critic*, 54.

as an auxiliary international language have often advanced as an argument in its favor the fact that the language is now spoken by over five million people. By this numerical standard, Chinese ought to stand a close second as an international language, since it is spoken by four hundred fifty million, or every fourth human being on earth. (55)

Here Lin also draws upon the work of philologists such as Otto Jespersen (who had inspired the Imagists), who regarded the Chinese language as the simplest, most advanced, and most logical language. Paraphrasing Jespersen's thesis in *Progress in Language*, Lin writes, "In fact, the whole trend of the development of the English language teaches us that it has been steadily advancing toward the Chinese type. English common sense has triumphed over grammatical nonsense and refused to see sex in a tea cup or a writing chair" (ibid.). In addition, there is an economic factor that will make pidgin the inevitable international language: the future of world commerce will be around the Pacific. In this case, Basic English, as is advocated by Ogden, which has not listed *ladies* or *gentlemen*, but only *men* and *women*, will simply not do, because "we know the future Pacific merchant will have to use the words 'ladies' and 'gentlemen' if he is not to go about referring to every lady as 'that woman' and lose his business" (58).

Continuing in his idiosyncratic lighthearted tone, Lin puts out his pidgin program to replace the purists' models:

> The trouble with Basic English is that it is not analytic enough. We find the word "gramophone," for instance, circumlocuted in Basic English as "a polished black disc with a picture of a dog in front of a horn." In 2400 A.D., we could call it more simply in real pidgin as "talking box." Basic English is still at a loss to express "telescope" and "microscope." In 2400, we shall call it more simply "look-far-glass" and "show-small-glass." We could dispense with the word "telegraph" (which is not in Basic) and call it "electric report," and replace "telephone" by the pidgin "electric talk." A "cinema" will then simply be "electric picture." And a "radio" will simply be "no-wire-electricity." (56–57)

We should bear in mind that all these pidgin expressions are literal translations from Chinese. Put in a different context—in Charlie Chan's mouth,
for instance—these Chinglish expressions would, to be sure, become examples of a debased tongue spoken by a debased race. But it is also interesting to see how closely these expressions resemble the version of Chinese
as promulgated by the Imagists and the related ethnographers, using either
Pound / Fenollosa's ideogrammic method or Lowell / Ayscough's analytic
method. We can compare Lin's "look-far-glass" and "no-wire-electricity"
with Pound / Fenollosa's "man standing by his word" *(sincerity)* and "the
sun caught in the tree" *(east)*, or with Lowell / Ayscough's "whirled water of
meeting streams" *(whirlpool)* and "calm with the leisure of moonlight
through an open door" *(leisure)*. In a strange way, Chinese as an ideal language and Chinese as an inferior tongue become mixed in Lin's Chinglish,
which in turn opens a horizon for the English language unimaginable from
the perspective of linguistic purists.

It is no wonder that Lin has often been undervalued by critics who
are bent on finding overtly politicized themes in literary works—Lin,
after all, very much prefers to write about his toothbrush rather than
current national issues. He wrote in the introduction to a collection of
his essays, "And now, looking back at the results of these years of casual
writing, I am glad that I did not write on the 'Fourth Plenary Session' or
the 'Arrival of Wang Chingwei at the North Station,' and that instead I
wrote on the Tooth-Brush. For a tooth-brush is a tooth-brush in 1935 as
in 1930, whereas my readers themselves will have forgotten what the
Fourth Plenary Session was all about, while the Naval Three-Year Plan
has, for all I know, gone to sleep. I have the audacity to hope, however,
that my readers will still be interested in my tooth-brush" (v–vi). But
this certainly does not mean that Lin was not concerned with national
politics. As Xiao-huang Yin keenly observes, many of Lin's writings
are often "highly political, angry, impassioned, and even rebellious"
("Worlds of Difference" 180). The problem is that it is very difficult to
tell when this master of humor is serious and when, if ever, he is being
plain funny. But such difficulty pertains to the essence of irony, to the

ironic position in which a bilingual writer such as Lin is situated. Especially when there are vastly different representations of the same culture, some naively idealistic, while others are ignorantly racist, a writer who picks his way through the messy bushes, avoiding not the thorns or knots but rather any clear-cut, simplistic logical outlet, will necessarily present a theoretical predicament for a positivistic history, one that, to quote Greenblatt again, "knows where it is going."[14] In the case of Lin, who says, "If I contradict myself here as a Chinese, I am happy as a Chinese that I contradict myself," we are stuck with the irony.

But irony will work, just as textual representations will make claims on us by their attempted claims on reality. A case in point is the second writer I discuss, who has participated in the cacophonic ensemble of representing the Chinese language—the contemporary Asian American poet John Yau. Whereas Imagists ventriloquize Chinese without parody and Biggers parodies its speakers through pidginization, John Yau follows the ventriloquism by further ventriloquizing it and parodies the pidginization by further pidginizing it.

As a poet, Yau grew up in a cultural environment in which literary Orientalism collided with outright racism. His relationship to Imagism, for example, is a complicated one. In an interview, he once stated:

> Certainly the Imagist Pound is something I read quite carefully
> when I first discovered him, but I went on to read *Personae*, which
> contained his *Cathay* poems, and I was certainly intrigued by them.
> Pound's Chinese poems were very, very meaningful to me then. I
> just read them over and over again . . . and I was reading the anthol-
> ogy of Imagist poets that William Pratt had edited in the sixties
> when I was first going to college, and I used those two things to
> teach myself how to write a poem. I used these books to imitate, you

---

14. Stephen Greenblatt, *Marvelous Possessions: The Wonder of the New World* (Chicago: University of Chicago Press, 1991), 2.

know. So I would imitate John Gould Fletcher and T. E. Hulme and H. D. and all the others.[15]

With his declared indebtedness to Imagism, Yau composes poems that seem to imitate Imagist ventriloquism, but his imitation itself contains another layer of ventriloquism, as in this one, entitled "From the Chinese" (1979), which is oddly reminiscent of the aforesaid Lowell's "From China":

> I put on your gown, and was comforted by its blue
> Tigers curling around me, even though it was dark.
> Sometimes, even the stars are hidden by their dutiful glow.
>
> Sometimes, even the stars are hidden by their dutiful glow,
> As only the moon trundles down the mountain path.
> But how was I to know why you got up, and stood by the open
> window?[16]

Compared with Lowell's poem, in which "I" directly assumes the role of a Chinese concubine, Yau's has a "you" standing between "I" and "the Chinese." And who is this "you"? Can it simply be an imaginary Chinese persona, since the scene is typically "Chinese," with blue gown, tigers, and the moon on mountain path? Or can it be a poetic persona, such as Lowell, who has imagined herself being in a "Chinese" scene? Or, in another poem, "Reflections" (previously quoted in chapter 3), Lowell identifies herself with a woman in "a rain-blue, silken gown":

> When I looked into your eyes,
> I saw a garden
> With peonies, and tinkling pagodas,
> And round-arched bridges
> Over still lakes.
> A woman sat beside the water
> In a rain-blue, silken garment.[17]

---

15. John Yau, "Interview with Edward Foster," *Talisman* 5 (1990): 43.
16. John Yau, *Sometimes* (New York: The Sheep Meadow Press, 1979), 54.
17. Amy Lowell, *Pictures of the Floating World* (New York: Macmillan, 1919), 27.

Both Lowell's poetic persona and this Chinese woman are, in turn, implied by Yau's "you": "I put on your gown, and was comforted by its blue." Yau seems to be mimicking Lowell's mimicking of Chinese, but his double mimicry in this case obviously lacks the parody permeating another series of his poems, poems that countermock Biggers's racist mocking.

This series is ironically entitled "Genghis Chan: Private Eye," collating Genghis Khan (the great Mongolian king who conquered half of the world in the thirteenth century) with Charlie Chan. And the poems themselves are also characterized by word collation and muddling, as in this one:

I posed
as a cookie
fortune smeller

I sold
the stale delays
your parents pranced to[18]

In response to the fortune-cookie Confucianism characteristic of Charlie Chan's speech, Yau plays with such characterization by muddling two phrases: fortune cookie and fortune teller. Since the fortune cookie is an American creation attributed to the Chinese, in fact it can never tell fortunes. Hence "I," seen as Chinese by "you" (recalling the "you" in "From the Chinese"), can only "pose," not as a fortune "teller," but as a "smeller." The identitarian masquerading implied in the word "pose" is also performed by the phonetic cross-dressing between "teller" and "smeller."

Sound play continues in another poem in the same series:

Grab some
Grub sum

Sub gum
machine stun

Treat pork
pig feet

18. John Yau, *Edificio Sayonara* (Santa Rosa, Calif.: Black Sparrow Press, 1989), 87.

On floor
all fours
Train cow
chow lane
Dice played
trade spice
Makes fist
first steps[19]

Marjorie Perloff, in her review of Yau's *Forbidden Entries*, has unpacked some of the word riddles for us, identifying puns and images that refer to the oldest of "Chinese" stereotypes: dim sum, chow mein, treated pork, the trained cow, the spice trade, the dice game, and the poor immigrant Chinese who must "Grab some / Grub sum," "make fist," and slave in factories ("machine stun").[20] "Yau is calling attention," Perloff summarizes, "to the lingering orientalism of U.S. culture, the labeling that continues to haunt Chinese-Americans."[21]

While Perloff is correct in her interpretation of the semantic force of this passage, there is another linguistic feature worth noting in Yau's poetry: his play with pidginization. Sound and spelling approximations between *grab* and *grub*, *sum* and *some*, *sum* and *sub*, *treat* and *feet*, *floor* and *fours*, *chow lane* and *chow mein*, *fist* and *first* are all characteristic of the kind of pidginization by which Oriental languages have been portrayed in American racist literature. It may recall, for instance, Charlie Chan's "Allight, boss." The muddling of words clearly imitates the floweriness and inscrutability of Charlie Chan's speech. Needless to say, what is involved in Yau's poems is an intentional play, a countermockery of the

19. John Yau, *Forbidden Entries* (Santa Rosa, Calif.: Black Sparrow Press, 1996), 102.

20. In his letter to the author, July 29, 1999, Yau wrote, "Sub gum machine stun = submachine gun (among other things). Didn't GI's always chew gum in the movies? And of course, in my childhood, the reruns of movies on TV that depicted World War II, and the Japanese, was one thread of music running through my mind."

21. Marjorie Perloff, review of *Forbidden Entries*, by John Yau, *Boston Review* 22.3–4 (1997): 39–41.

mockery of Charlie Chan, just as the title of the series, "Genghis Chan," contains an explicit double irony. Better still, the format in which many poems in this series are composed also suggests a parody: short couplets or triplets, which may be seen as pidginized versions of Japanese haiku or Chinese classical lyrics. In this case, one cannot even tell whether Yau parodies only the racist stereotypes in American pop culture or if he also mocks, to paraphrase Perloff, the lingering U.S. *literary* Orientalism, in which the Imagists—or even maybe the earlier Yau who followed them—participated.

However, this distinction is not as important as what we have learned so far regarding racial identity and language. It is true that a language, especially in its pidginized form, may be tied to a stereotyped racial identity, and thus a literary work's concern with language may fall back to racial questions, as in the case of Biggers's Charlie Chan. Or as often seen in minority literatures, there is a strategy of associating a language or dialect with a racial identity to promote ethnic interests. However, the value of the latter lies in breaking from the dominant, standard language practice, rather than in creating another "natural" tie between language and identity. In fact, as in Imagism, the obsession with the racial Other's language stays inside the realm of linguistic culture, the *racial* association being rarely foregrounded. Yau's work, especially, through ventriloquizing Imagism's ventriloquism and pidginizing racist literature's pidginization of Chinese, problematizes rather than foregrounds language's ties to racial identity. And the countermockery and double mimicry in Yau's poetry further complicate the cross-cultural displacement taking place in language, a displacement to whose other routes I now turn.

FIVE

Maxine Hong Kingston and the Making of an "American" Myth

The old people in a new world, the new people made
out of the old, that is the story that I mean to tell, for
that is what really is and what I really know.

Gertrude Stein, The Making of Americans

Compared to Lin Yutang and John Yau, who are ambivalent about their ironic intercultural positions, another Asian American writer, Maxine Hong Kingston, is evidently more committed to a notion of American-ness. Regarding her first book, *The Woman Warrior* (1975), Kingston insisted, "I'm not even saying that those are Chinese myths anymore. I'm saying I've written American myths. Fa Mulan and the writing on her back is an American myth."[1] Kingston declared of her second book, *China Men* (1980), that her goal was to "reclaim America." And in her third book, *Tripmaster Monkey: His Fake Book* (1989), the hero Wittman Ah Sing is named after a poet of quintessential "American" spirit, Walt

1. Quoted in Jeffery Chan et al., eds., *The Big Aiiieeeee! An Anthology of Chinese American and Japanese American Literature* (New York: Meridian, 1991), 50.

Whitman.[2] The 1998 release of the Walt Disney film *Mulan* especially fulfilled Kingston's prophecy on the Americanness of her character Mulan: in the film, what was originally a Chinese story about a girl who went to war in place of her aging father becomes an American myth, one in which a young woman struggles to achieve her individuality—to realize, as Mulan says in the film, what her "worth" is.

Actually, Mulan's American transformation started with Kingston's *The Woman Warrior,* where the story of Mulan is conflated with that of another Chinese hero, Yue Fei. This transplantation and others in the book immediately drew criticism from many Asian American writers. Among them, Frank Chin delivered the harshest critique, accusing Kingston of "faking" Chinese myths. In an article entitled "Come All Ye Asian American Writers of the Real and the Fake," Chin maintained that "myths are, by nature, immutable and unchanging because they are deeply ingrained in the cultural memory, or they are not myths" (29). To prove Kingston's fakery, he reprinted in his provocative article a Chinese version of "The Ballad of Mulan" along with an English translation, as if to say that *this* is the real Chinese story of Mulan. But little did Chin know that this ballad was not "Chinese" in the first place. And contrary to his belief, not only do myths undergo constant revision and transformation—and hence as Aristotle suggested in *Poetics*, "We must not at all costs keep to the received legends" (9.8)—but also a culture or nation never ceases to change its self-definition or boundary. Therefore, it is necessary that we temporarily bracket concepts that suggest homogene-

2. In the context of the long-established racist convention of calling Chinese characters by such names as "Ah Sing" and "Ah Sin," one could legitimately claim that Kingston's naming of her character in this case constitutes a textual gesture analogous to John Yau's "Genghis Chan," which I have understood as a countermockery. There is no denying that Kingston's work embodies a powerful critique of the racist, exclusionist versions of Americanness. But my current questioning of her commitment to a notion of Americanness is based on an understanding of the politics of literary form and linguistic practice, which relies less on what the literary work says thematically than what it does in the context of writing and reading as sociological practices. See my further discussion of this in light of Bernstein's and Guillory's critiques of the new canon, following.

ity (e.g., *China, Chinese, culture,* and *origin*) when we are dealing with a truly transnational phenomenon, such as Mulan.

And this is where the pitfall lies in Kingston's claim to Americanness. For what is an "American" myth? What is so "American" about it? Certainly, when Kingston says emphatically that "I am an American. I am an American writer, who, like other American writers, wants to write the great American novel," it must be granted that her insistence on Americanness can be understood as a politically motivated gesture; one made in the interest of reclaiming the rights of citizenship denied to ethnic minorities and rejecting the ghettoization of ethnic writings as a subgroup of American literature.[3] However, just as citizenship requires "naturalization" and a pledge of allegiance, membership in the American literary canon comes at the price of conformity, which is manifested probably less in the themes that literary works express than in the orthodox, normalized ways the writing is produced. As a vital part of the social mechanism of signification, writing is often controlled through the establishment of stylistic conventions and standardization of forms.[4] As I argue in this chapter, what is perhaps most profoundly "American" about Kingston's work are the ways in which stories like "Mulan" are transformed and the ways in which this transformation is interpreted by literary scholars. Both the transformation and its interpretation exemplify a linguistic positivism shared by canonical American literature and Asian American literature in its current formation. It is this shared conception of language that brings Kingston closer to the American literary canon and makes her work truly "American."

3. Maxine Hong Kingston, "Cultural Mis-Reading by American Reviewers," in *Asian and Western Writers in Dialogue: New Cultural Identities,* ed. Guy Amirthanayagam (London: Macmillan, 1982), 57–58.

4. Many modern cultural critics, including Antonio Gramsci, Louis Althusser, Mikhail Bakhtin, and Julia Kristeva, have argued eloquently for the significance of literary form as an expression of cultural hegemony and as a site for social resistance. For more contemporary discussions of the issue, see Charles Bernstein, ed., *The Politics of Poetic Form: Poetry and Public Policy* (New York: Roof Books, 1990), and John Guillory, *Cultural Capital: The Problem of Literary Canon Formation* (Chicago: University of Chicago Press, 1993).

The word "canon" refers not only to the controlled process of select-ing a body of "great" works, but also to the dominant methodology of reading and interpretation that accompanies the selections. It seems that the contemporary literature of the United States has been polarized in such a way that on the one side stand the guardians of "the Western Canon," such as Harold Bloom, and on the other, the culturalists, his-toricists, and multiculturalists. To use Bloom's own metaphor, the situa-tion may best be described as "heights versus numbers."[5] Yet, despite the apparent polarity, the two sides in fact stand at the same pole. As Charles Bernstein pointed out in his keynote address at the 1992 NEMLA Convention, "Indeed, cultural and multicultural studies offer a revitalized version of the traditional humanities, which have suffered from near asphyxiation by means of the anti-democratic arguments for the received authority of a narrow band of cultural arbiters. Far from challenging the legitimating process of the university, the cultural stud-ies movement actually extends this process in ways that are largely con-sonant with a tradition that comes to us in fits and starts from the Enlightenment's attack on Scholasticism."[6] What both the old and new canons share, Bernstein argues, are the Enlightenment and Romantic principles of critical self-reflection and disinterested observation.

John Guillory, in his brilliant analysis of literary canon formation, also suggests that cultural and multicultural studies have not presented a real challenge to the old canon. The reason for this, he argues, is that by pro-posing the question of representation of social identity as their basis for the critique of the canon, the "new" models have failed to understand canon formation as "a problem in the constitution and distribution of cul-tural capital, or more specifically, a problem of access to the means of lit-

5. See Harold Bloom's article, entitled "They Have the Number; We, the Heights," *Boston Review* 23.2 (April/May 1998): 24–29.

6. Charles Bernstein's speech, entitled "What's Art Got to Do with It?: The Status of the Subject of the Humanities in an Age of Cultural Studies," is now collected in his book *My Way: Speeches and Poems* (Chicago: University of Chicago Press, 1999); for the quota-tion, see p. 37.

erary production and consumption." Guillory posits that as the institutional means of disseminating knowledge, the literary syllabus in schools constitutes cultural capital in two senses: linguistic capital ("the means by which one attains a socially credentialed and therefore valued speech, otherwise known as 'Standard English'") and symbolic capital ("a kind of knowledge-capital whose possession can be displayed upon request and which thereby entitles its possessor to the cultural and material rewards of the well-educated person"). He then comes to an incisive conclusion: "These two kinds of capital [are] ultimately more socially significant in their effects than the 'ideological' content of literary works, a content which the critics of the canon see as reinforcing the exclusion of minority authors from the canon by expressing the same values which determine exclusionary judgments. Literary works must be seen rather as the vector of ideological notions which do not inhere in the works themselves but in the context of their institutional presentation, or more simply, in the way in which they are taught."[7] In light of Guillory's concept of cultural capital, in this chapter I focus on the linguistic and symbolic aspects of the writing and reading (Guillory's "production and consumption") of Kingston's work and thereby demonstrate how the deeply rooted linguistic positivism of the Western literary tradition perpetuates itself in the wake of multicultural recanonization and prevents the formation of radical, transnational models of American literary studies.

As manifested in language and literature, positivism assumes an isomorphic relation between the word and the world and promotes the semantics of objective referentiality over the poetic, nonreferential dimensions in language. It suggests that there is an extralinguistic experience—American or not—that can be captured and represented by literature regardless of the particularity of the mediating language.[8] In

---

7. Guillory, *Cultural Capital*, ix.

8. Standing at the opposite pole is of course linguistic relativism, which endorses the belief that our understanding of the world is conditioned by our own linguistic structure and that there are certain things peculiar to our particular language. As Edward Sapir, the major theoretician of linguistic relativism, put it: "The fact of the matter is that the 'real

literature, this positivistic principle has a corollary that is easy to identify. Most canonical and ethnic literary studies focus on thematization, and the literary works chosen as subjects of study are mostly narrative texts that might yield coherent, abstracted themes. This is especially so in ethnic literature, where studies often focus on the representation of the so-called ethnic or immigrant experience while the particularity of the ethnic languages or dialects mediating the experience is to a various degree ignored. One of the symptoms of this narrowness of focus is the recent increase in the use of personal narratives as textbooks for grade-school and college literature courses. Such a predilection for "gripping" personal narratives may be analyzed in light of what Bernstein has called "the artifice of absorption." In a poetic treatise, Bernstein analyzes the inner workings of realism that relies on a central technique of transparency and absorption, by which he means the various textual strategies and their intended aesthetic effects—engrossing, engulfing completely, engaging, arresting attention, reverie, attention intensification, rhap-

---

world' is to a large extent unconsciously built up on the language habits of the group. No two languages are ever sufficiently similar to be considered as representing the same social reality. The worlds in which different societies live are distinct worlds, not merely the same world with different labels attached" (*Selected Writings of Edward Sapir in Language, Culture and Society*, ed. D. G. Mandelbaum [Berkeley and Los Angeles: University of California Press, 1949], 162). A position similar to Sapir's has been formulated by another linguistic anthropologist, Paul Friedrich, in *The Language Parallax: Linguistic Relativism and Poetic Indeterminacy* (Austin: University of Texas Press, 1986). Friedrich emphasizes the poetic, indeterminate aspects of language, maintaining that poetic language "is the locus of the most interesting differences between languages and should be the focus of the study of such differences" (17), because "the poetic potential of language—not logic or basic reference—most massively determines the imagination" (43). However, the limitations to relativism become obvious when it assumes a homogeneous linguistic-cultural identity for the speakers of a language. It is true that there are structures in a language that can be a binding force in shaping one's world—or, as Hans-Georg Gadamer puts it, "structures that constitute one's prejudice" (*Truth and Method*, 2d, rev. ed., trans. Joel Weinsheimer and Donald G. Marshall [New York: Continuum, 1995], 269–77). But relativism fails to recognize the differences that are always at work inside (if there were an "inside") linguistic cultures. Given the cross-cultural and multilingual character of Asian American literature—or, in fact, any literature—a linguistic relativism based on the particularity of a single language practice is no longer sufficient to account for it.

sodic, spellbinding, mesmerizing, hypnotic, total, riveting, enthralling.[9] Part of what such absorptive realism achieves, Bernstein states quoting Ford Madox Ford, is that it "will give you more the sense of having been present at an event than if you had actually been corporally present" (27). In this way, the narrative presents "an unmediated (immediate) experience of facts, either of the 'external' world of nature or the 'internal' world of the mind" by calling attention away from its artifice (9).

In Asian American literature, in particular, the generic preference for realist, personal narratives is too obvious for anyone to miss. From Sui Sin Far to Younghill Kang, Jade Snow Wong, Louis Chu, John Okada, Maxine Hong Kingston, and Amy Tan, the writers' representative works (as determined by the canon makers) are predominantly prose narratives—whether memoir, autobiography, biography, novel, or short story. In current Asian American literary studies, a focus on narratives is also dominant, as evidenced by journal essays, conference papers, graduate theses, and book-length studies.[10] Interestingly, in works that are intended to establish a canon in Asian American literature, scholars often acknowledge their generic preference, but they give personal excuses that may only prevent further probing into the problem of genre.[11] Take

---

9. Charles Bernstein, *A Poetics* (Cambridge: Harvard University Press, 1992), 29.

10. In a recent essay on Asian American poetry, Juliana Chang noted that "beginning in the late 1970s and early 1980s . . . prose fiction became a prevalent means of circulating narratives of racial difference among a larger audience" ("Reading Asian American Poetry," *MELUS* 21.1 [1996]: 81). However, by criticizing the generic preference for prose narrative in Asian American literature, I am by no means insinuating that other genres, such as poetry, may be *generically* less susceptible to the problems of linguistic positivism. In fact, the mode of single-voiced narrative, often found in the work of canonized Asian American poets such as Li-Young Lee, Cathy Song, and Garrett Hongo, is subject to the critique I am presenting here. Ultimately, the problem does not lie in genre but in the understanding of the nature of language. But in this chapter, I address the problems of prose narrative first, since it is still the prevalent genre in Asian American literature.

11. An important exception even within studies that focus mainly on narratives, one that deals closely and sufficiently with the poetic and figurative—that is, less positivistic— dimensions of prose narrative, is King-Kok Cheung's *Articulate Silences: Hisaye Yamamoto, Maxine Hong Kingston, Joy Kogawa* (Ithaca: Cornell University Press, 1993). Lisa Lowe, in

for instance, Sau-ling Cynthia Wong's *Reading Asian American Literature: From Necessity to Extravagance* (1993). Wong declares in her introduction:

> My primary sources are mostly prose narratives—novels, novellas, autobiographies, short stories—because, *relative to works in other genres, they are likely to exhibit more readily discernible linkages to the extratextual world and are therefore more amenable to my project.* Personal inclination is also a factor: not only have my training and research interests always been in fiction but, given the rapidly increasing size and variety of the Asian American corpus, I feel a multigenre study would simply be beyond my powers.[12]

If someone prefers spaghetti to rice, there is nothing to say about her personal choice of diet. But if she adds that spaghetti is more nutritious than rice, then there is a possibility for a debate, since the claim is now depersonalized. So also with the disclaimer made by Wong. What seems to be private has in fact entered the domain of the public. Wong's statement that prose narratives "are likely to exhibit more readily discernible linkages to the extratextual world" indicates a problematic larger than a personal disclaimer contains.

To illustrate how readily prose narratives yield an apparent isomorphism between the word and the world, let's take Wong's thematic reading of Kingston's work. In the following passage, Wong reads *The Woman Warrior* without any consideration of language's mediating function:

> Why does she end up championing the cause of the no-name woman, whom she condemns energetically with her conscious mind? In what ways is she like the prodigal, so that she can empathize with her sufferings? Of course, Brave Orchid, *typical of the women of the seafaring regions of Guangdong from which many early Chinese-Americans originated,* has

---

Immigrant Acts: On Asian American Cultural Politics (Durham: Duke University Press, 1996), has also presented in her reading of *Dictée* by Theresa Cha and other poetic texts a very powerful argument for the political significance of form.

12. Sau-ling Cynthia Wong, *Reading Asian American Literature: From Necessity to Extravagance* (Princeton: Princeton University Press, 1993), 12; emphasis added.

herself been a left-at-home "Gold Mountain wife" for many years. Like Moon Orchid's husband, "year after year," Maxine's father "did not come home or send for her," but "did send money regularly." In the meantime, she had to be the dutiful daughter-in-law and serve her husband's "tyrant mother." For fully two decades she lives as a "widow of the living." (*Reading* 199; emphasis added)

Mikhail Bakhtin would call this reading a "philosophical monologization," which he defines as either "a passionate philosophizing with the characters" or "a dispassionate psychological or psychopathological analysis of them as objects." According to Bakhtin, both approaches are "equally incapable of penetrating the special artistic architectonics" of literary works.[13] The typology of "the women of the seafaring regions of Guangdong," in particular, transfers Wong's reading smoothly and immediately from "the plane of the novel" to "the plane of reality" (20). And such reading exactly attests to the insightfulness of Guillory's remark that "the typical valorization of the noncanonical author's experience as a marginalized social identity necessarily reasserts the transparency of the text to the experience it represents" (10). It is true that Wong does mention some of the "postmodern" techniques used in the narrative, such as "syntactic cues suggesting conjecture," but even this momentary attention to writing merely serves to illustrate the "theme" she attempts to grasp.[14] What remains essential in her reading is the unmediated reference to the phenomenal, extralinguistic world.

Kingston's work invites such a reading. Indeed, her first two books were published as nonfiction and won the National Book Award for that category. The nonfiction designation implies that there are real-life stories behind the books and that interpretations could be made in relation to these stories, independent of the language that constitutes them.

13. Mikhail Bakhtin, *Problems of Dostoevsky's Poetics*, ed. and trans. Caryl Emerson (Minneapolis: University of Minnesota Press, 1984), 9.

14. Sau-ling Cynthia Wong, "Necessity and Extravagance in Maxine Hong Kingston's *The Woman Warrior*," *MELUS* 15.1 (1988): 8.

When Kingston's third book was published as a novel, Patricia Lin, who has thematically interpreted her earlier work with a positivist slant,[15] suggests that the new book be read not as a novel but as an ethnography:

> The argument for reading *Tripmaster Monkey* as an ethnographic
> enterprise of the postmodern era rather than as a novel is based
> on the premise that it "anthropologizes" rather than novelizes the
> United States. In other words, ethnography exposes the constitution
> of everyday or taken for granted realities.[16]

To substantiate her argument, Lin draws heavily upon the ground-breaking anthology of essays in anthropology (briefly discussed earlier)—that is, *Writing Culture: The Poetics and Politics of Ethnography*, edited by James Clifford and George Marcus. But Lin has in fact misunderstood the theoretical orientations of the anthology and thus perpetuated the positivist principle in literature.

When Lin contrasts ethnography with the novel, she is obviously insinuating that ethnography is a realistic representation of reality, whereas a novel only "simulate[s] the actual" ("Clashing" 335). Even when she agrees with Fredric Jameson that "in the postmodern era, what is finally left for the artist is the task of re-presenting representations," or when she claims that "this is a world . . . that is preinhabited and defined by mythologies, stereotypes, and cultural constructs," she still reads *Tripmaster Monkey* as a book that represents a world thus characterized (337). This representational model runs exactly counter to the theoretical premise put forward by the editors of *Writing Culture:* "[The] focus on text making and rhetoric serves to highlight the constructed, artificial nature of cultural accounts. . . . [Ethnography] is always caught up in the

15. See Patricia Lin's essay, "The Icicle in the Desert: Perspective and Form in the Works of Two Chinese American Women Writers," *MELUS* 6.3 (1979): 51–71.

16. Patricia Lin, "Clashing Constructs of Reality: Reading Maxine Hong Kingston's *Tripmaster Monkey: His Fake Book* as Indigenous Ethnography," in *Reading Literatures of Asian America*, ed. Shirley Geok-Lin Lim and Amy Ling (Philadelphia: Temple University Press, 1992), 335.

invention, not representation, of culture" (2). Contrary to Lin's understanding that "new ethnography mirrors the postmodern condition in its
efforts to represent the multiplicity of human existence using a much
wider range of discourses than the approved scientific, textual, and
empirical approaches," the main thrust of *Writing Culture* does not lie in
finding new ways for ethnographic representation, but rather in its prob-
lematizing of representation itself ("Clashing" 335). It questions not only
the old ways of representation, but also the very possibility of doing representational ethnography. The old truth claim made by ethnography is
questioned because its textual and *fictional* nature is being recognized. In
this way, the borderline between ethnography and fiction is blurred.
Therefore, Lin's reading of *Tripmaster Monkey* as a work that "anthropol-
ogizes" rather than novelizes stands on a mistaken premise. Consequently, her otherwise promising study becomes another positivistic
treatment of literature. Still, her recognition of the realist ethnographic
intent in Kingston's work is insightful, because the work does solicit such
interpretations.

Kingston's *The Woman Warrior* is, from the very beginning, filled
with intrigues and problematics of ethnography:

> "You must not tell anyone," my mother said, "what I am about to
> tell you. In China your father had a sister who killed herself. She
> jumped into the family well. We say that your father has all brothers
> because it is as if she had never been born." (3)

The narrator establishes the authenticity of the story by revealing to
us a taboo, something that her mother did not allow her to tell. It is
true that this mother would later undermine the veracity of her own
stories by ridiculing the narrator for being unable to tell a story from
a real event, but the reader is already framed into the "real" event, that
is, "my mother said." Such framing strikingly parallels the "arrival"
trope often used in ethnography. In an ethnographic work that
intends to interpret a culture, the objectified description and scientific
analysis are often combined with a personal narrative that usually

comes at the very beginning of the book. The narrative tells of the ethnographer's arrival in the field, becoming present in a culture that lives in the past.[17] Likewise, in Kingston's book, the validity of the description or imagination of past events is predicated on a personal narrative laid out in the very beginning: "My mother said." And better still, the implied "my" presence comes before "mother," who *was* once present in China.

At this point *The Woman Warrior* still seems to stand on the solid ground of reality. Kingston had prepared herself to ward off criticisms that she has engaged in "fakery" by using outside source materials. Whatever took place in the textual world could now be attributed to the real world. Kingston would later attempt to justify her "inaccurate" usage of Chinese legends by characterizing first-generation Chinese Americans ("mother" included) as being forgetful: "They forgot a lot of the myths. Many changed myths because they had new adventures. Many changed myths to explain their new situations they were having."[18] It was in response to this self-justification that Chin insisted that "myths are, by nature, immutable and unchanging because they are deeply ingrained in the cultural memory, or they are not myths." While the limitation to Chin's notion of "immutable and unchanging" cultural texts is easily discernible, Kingston's positivism is camouflaged by the seemingly commonsensical notion that she tells the story the way reality dictates. Both Kingston and her interpreters jump to the conclusion that the fractures in the stories are dictated by the fractures in reality. In so doing, they ignore the fact that stories are often intertextual variants of one another. As Roland Barthes writes, "The text is a tissue of quotations drawn from the innumerable centres of culture.... The writer can only imitate a gesture that is always anterior, never

17. Mary Louise Pratt presents a brilliant analysis of this "arrival" trope often used in ethnography in her essay "Fieldwork in Common Places" in *Writing Culture: The Poetics and Politics of Ethnography*, ed. James Clifford and George Marcus (Berkeley and Los Angeles: University of California Press, 1986), 27–50.

18. Chan et al., *The Big Aiiieeeee!*, 29.

original."[19] Indeed, stories are often filled with fractures resulting from intertextual travels, and these fractures may remain to haunt positivistic approaches to literature.

While Kingston can attempt to establish the veracity of her novel through an ethnographic trope that is predicated on a personal narrative, she can no longer do so with the stories, legends, and myths that she has borrowed. The example that immediately comes to mind is the notorious conflation, in *The Woman Warrior*, of the Fa Mulan legend and the Yue Fei story. Here is the passage on Fa Mulan:[20]

> After I grew up, I heard the chant of Fa Mu Lan, the girl who took her father's place in battle. Instantly I remembered that as a child I had followed my mother about the house, the two of us singing about how Fa Mu Lan fought gloriously and returned alive from war to settle in the village. I had forgotten this chant that was once mine, given me by my mother, who may not have known its power to remind. She said I would grow up a wife and a slave, but she taught me the song of the woman warrior, Fa Mu Lan. I would have to grow up a woman warrior. (20)

A dozen pages later, after an imaginary ordeal of "myself" as a woman warrior, which is largely based on the framework of the Chinese Fa Mulan ballad itself, scenes from the Yue Fei story are almost seamlessly stitched into the woman warrior narrative:

> My mother put a pillow on the floor before the ancestors. "Kneel here," she said. "Now take off your shirt." I kneeled with my back to my parents so none of us felt embarrassed. My mother washed my back as if I had left for only a day and were her baby yet. "We are going to carve revenge on your back," my father said. "We'll write out oaths and names." (34)

19. Roland Barthes, *Image, Music, Text*, trans. Stephen Heath (New York: Hill and Wang, 1977), 146.

20. Fa Mulan, Fa Mu Lan, Hua Mulan, and Hua Mu Lan are all variations of the same name.

Both Fa Mulan and Yue Fei are characters from Chinese legends known to every household. Fa Mulan is a woman warrior who wore men's clothes, took her father's place when he was drafted, and became a heroine in the war. Yue Fei is a male patriotic marshal who defended China against the Jin invasion, and his mother carved four characters on his back as a motto: *jing zhong bao guo*, "Be loyal and avenge your nation."

What is interesting and crucial here is the transformation these two stories have gone through in relation to the constantly changing boundary of Chinese culture and especially in relation to each other. The Fa Mulan ballad is "originally" a folk song of a nomad tribe that lived to the north of China around the fifth century A.D. The song itself may be about a war against China, which would make Fa Mulan a heroine in an anti-China war. But, contrary to Chin's assertion about "immutable and unchangeable" cultural texts, the song was later copied down, translated into Chinese, and revised numerous times in the hands of anonymous Chinese scribes and scholars. As a result of this transcultural migration, there are many instances of anachronism and contradiction in the extant versions of this chant.[21] In comparison, the Yue Fei story is much simpler, since in the very beginning it was told as a Chinese tale about a patriotic hero fighting against a nomad tribe from the north. Interestingly, the embedded antithesis between these two stories has been allowed to cohabit inside a vaguely defined "Chinese" cultural narrative, although the rupture is always there.[22]

If we think of culture as a text constituted by many intertexts—commensurate or incommensurate—then Fa Mulan and Yue Fei are just two incommensurate intertexts. When they are transposed to Kingston's

21. Jinan Daxue Zhongwenxi, ed., *Zhongguo Lidai Shige Mingpian Shangxi* (Changsha, China: Hunan Renming Chubanshe, 1983), 182.

22. Just as the idea of "America" has been used as a means of cultural assimilation, "China" has also been defined as a center that absorbs different ethnic groups and cultural narratives into the homogeneous "Middle Kingdom." Thus, my critique of the "Americanness" implied in Kingston's work is also a critique of "Chineseness," or of any formation of a homogeneous cultural identity that eliminates differences.

text they carry over this antithesis, for anyone who is informed of it will always read the woman warrior story with a double vision. Focused vision can be created only when the text strives to hegemonize the intertexts by presenting a narrowly defined theme. In fact, Kingston's text does attempt to conceal the discrepancy, as is evident in one simple textual maneuver. Although the description of the tattooing scene is full of elaborate details, the text never yields what has been written on the woman warrior's back, except in the father's vague statement: "We are going to carve revenge on your back....We'll write out oaths and names" (34). The indeterminacy seems deliberate, for as soon as the exact words were given out, the fracture between the two intertexts would become too wide for the narrator to conceal, and the reader who knows both stories would be able to recognize the inaccuracy.

Compared with *The Woman Warrior,* Kingston's second book, *China Men* (1980), relies even more heavily on transposing Chinese intertexts. To run a short list: (1) "On Discovery" is taken out of an eighteenth-century Chinese novel, *Flowers in the Mirror;* (2) "The Father from China" has an episode in which Father "reenacted" ancient Chinese scholars' anecdotes; (3) "The Ghostmate" is an adaptation of a well-known Chinese ghost story; (4) "The Adventure of Lo Bun Sun" is a back-translation from the Chinese version of *Robinson Crusoe;* (5) "The Li Sao: An Elegy" relies heavily—to the point of plagiarizing—on Kuo Mojo's "A Sketch of Ch'u Yuan."[23] The second item, the chapter "The Father from China," is an example that illustrates Kingston's intertextual maneuver. Here BaBa, the father, is locked up in a closet to be prepared for the qualifying test for the Imperial Examination in China:

> BaBa sat on the cot, sat at the table....A jailer brought food,
> returned for the utensils, gave him back his bedroll, and locked him
> up "until time for the first test," he said. He left a teapot, around
> which BaBa held his hands and caught the rich heat that arose. He

23. See Qing-yun Wu's essay "A Chinese Reader's Response to Maxine Hong Kingston's *China Men,*" *MELUS* 17.3 (1991–92): 85–94.

decided to stay awake all night. The tea lasted a short while. Fireflies
in a jar would have given an appearance of warmth. Back in the village he had read by their light. . . . Muttering the texts, he gave voice
and breath to word after word. . . . He tried holding his eyelids open
with his fingers. . . . He stood on the chair and stretched—and felt a
hook or a ring in a beam directly overhead. . . . He looped the end of
his pigtail into the ring and tied it tight. Then he sat in his chair to
study some more. When he dozed, his own hair jerked his head back
up. Hours later, when the pull on his scalp no longer kept him alert,
he opened the table drawer, where he found an awl. Like the poets
whose blood had been wiped off it, he jabbed the awl into his thigh,
held it there, and studied on. (*China Men* 26)

As Qing-yun Wu correctly points out, there are three details here that
in fact come from well-known Chinese stories:

Ju Yin of the Jin (265–420) was too poor to buy lamp-oil and used a
bag of fireflies for reading. Sun Jing of the Han (206 B.C.–A.D. 220)
tied his pigtail to a beam to keep awake. During the period of the
Warring States (475–221 B.C.), Su Jin . . . studied military books day
and night. Once when he was too sleepy to keep his eyes open, he
thrust an awl into his thigh. Inspirited by the oozing blood and acute
pain, he continued reading.[24]

The issue here is not whether these are just allusions or outright plagiarism. Rather, what's at stake is whether they are all instances of intertextual transposition denied as such. The way in which BaBa's life becomes
blended with classical anecdotes is so smooth in Kingston's work that the
transposition is almost unnoticeable. To avoid the dichotomy of allusion
versus plagiarism (or "faking," as Chin puts it), I want to introduce the
term *translation*. As a crucial intertextual strategy, translation is transparent in Kingston's narrative. The Chinese source materials, when translated into English and used to constitute BaBa's life, have lost their mark-

24. Ibid., 87.

ers as foreign texts. Instead, they become representations of "strange" experiences to a reader who is not aware of the ongoing translation.[25]

The paradoxical combination of the incomprehensible strangeness of the foreign experience and the transparency of the language in which such strangeness is described constitutes one of the mainstays of Orientalism. Similarly, Kingston's work on the one hand attempts to represent Asian American experiences by drawing upon source materials that are foreign to an English-language reader, and on the other eradicates the foreign linguistic features in those intertexts by producing a fluent style of narrative in translation. In his excellent study of the history and politics of translation, Lawrence Venuti notes, "The illusion of transparency is an effect of fluent discourse, of the translator's effort to insure easy readability by adhering to current usage, maintaining continuous syntax, fixing a precise meaning."[26] Read as either a cultural translation or a textual translation, Kingston's re-presentation of Chinese intertexts tends to smooth away the linguistic ruptures resultant from intertextual / intercultural transposition.

This textual gesture is often ignored in the aesthetic appreciation of Kingston's work. Critics do talk about the so-called postmodern strategies used in her writing: "The various stories...are written in a variety of modes: realistic, satirical, allegorical, heroic, comic, tragi-comic, journalistic, and fabled. Fluidity replaces conventional form, and juxtaposition remains the only consistent narrative device. The range of materials and styles, quirky unpredictability of narrative movement, and disturbing juxtapositions imply an authorial mind at work."[27] But, Shirley Geok-Lin Lim, the same critic who lavishes this praise on Kingston, goes on to devalue another Asian American work, Louis Chu's *Eat a Bowl of Tea:* "The novel is by no means a successful work. Chu's writing is stilted, full of clichés and

25. See the next chapter for a more detailed discussion of the politics of translation.

26. Lawrence Venuti, *The Translator's Invisibility: A History of Translation* (New York: Routledge, 1995), 1.

27. Shirley Geok-Lin Lim, "Twelve Asian American Writers: In Search of Self-Definition," *MELUS* 13.1–2 (1986): 69.

clumsy constructions, pointing to the difficulties of a writer to whom English is still a second language" (ibid. 66). Such a bias against linguistic features resulting from textual / cultural translation lies at the heart of the new canonization of American literature in the wake of the surge of ethnic writings. What can be and is being accepted into the canon are mostly ethnic writings that conform to standard language practice. What hides behind these moves is, again, a positivistic assumption that there is a life experience (of immigrants and the white middle class alike) that can be represented in a universal language—in this case, standard English. The cultural translation of a universal "American" experience is thus reified, as Venuti argues, in the textual translation that eliminates the foreign, nonstandard elements of language experience. Hence the striking statement that ends *The Woman Warrior:* "It translated well" (*Woman Warrior* 209).

In recent decades, the decline of bilingual education in the United States has gone hand in hand with the increase in the use of ethnic personal narratives written in standard English for textbooks in grade schools and colleges. And many ethnic writers themselves endorse the English-only policy and carry out monolingualism in their work.[28] Kingston, for example, often teases the English reader with translations of Chinese characters and thematizes the ideographs, but, with only one or two exceptions in her three books, does not give the actual words. For example, in *The Woman Warrior,*

> The Chinese "I" has seven strokes, intricacies. How could the
> American "I," assuredly wearing a hat like the Chinese, have only

28. In a very important anthology, *Multilingual America: Transnationalism, Ethnicity, and the Languages of American Literature* (New York: New York University Press, 1998), the editor Werner Sollors records an interesting but disturbing incident in Asian American literary studies: "Literary histories, critical studies, anthologies, and even bibliographies of literature of the United States nowadays inevitably present English-only materials and often imply a monolingual Anglophone reader. A representative example of the 'natural' way in which this exclusion takes place can be found in *Asian-American Literature: An Annotated Bibliography*, a comprehensive work of nearly three hundred pages published under the auspices of the Modern Language Association, which includes the following, telling declaration of limits: '[W]e exclude works written in Asian languages, unless they have been translated into English'" (6).

three strokes, the middle so straight? Was it out of politeness that
this writer left off strokes the way a Chinese has to write her own
name small and crooked? ... The other troublesome word was
"here," no strong consonant to hang on to, and so flat, when "here"
is two mountainous ideographs. (166–67)

The Chinese characters would have interrupted the linear flow of self-
reflection and thematization and would also have fragmented the text,
making it more opaque and unfamiliar.[29]

From this perspective, the canonization of Kingston's work in American literature comes as no surprise, since her writing attempts to appropriate Chinese-language experience into her heavily standardized prose
narrative. In this respect, it may be worthwhile to compare Kingston
with a different writer, one whose colossal amount of innovative writing
is still undervalued by the canon: Gertrude Stein. A child of Jewish immigrants, Stein constantly questions the idea of ethnicity and identity, and
challenges language's capability to construct a positivistic identity. In one
of her works that supposedly addresses the issue of Americanization, *The
Making of Americans* (1925), Stein consciously constructs, in Werner Sollors's words, a "counterpiece to the realistic and semiautobiographical
novels one might expect from its title."[30] Take for instance the following
passage from the book:

The old people in a new world, the new people made out of the old,
that is the story that I mean to *tell*, for that is what *really* is and what
I *really know*.

29. Here I do not rule out the possibility that in her manuscript Kingston might have
put in the Chinese characters but the publisher decided to delete them to make the text
monolingual and "uncontaminated." Yet, as my analysis shows, Kingston's textual practice
is largely consistent with that of contemporary American publishers. See the next chapter
for a detailed discussion of the politics of the "fluent" and "uncontaminated" styles.

30. Werner Sollors, *Beyond Ethnicity: Consent and Descent in American Culture* (New
York: Oxford University Press, 1986), 255.

Some of the fathers we must *realize* so that we can *tell* our story
really, were little boys then, and they came across the water with
their parents, the grandparents we need only just remember. Some
of these our fathers and our mothers, were not even made then, and
the women, the young mothers, our grandmothers we perhaps just
have seen once, carried these our fathers and our mothers into the
new world inside them, those women of the old world strong to bear
them. Some looked very weak and little women, but even these so
weak and little, were strong always, to bear many children.[31]

The awkward, almost "foreign" sentence structures mediate and enact
the narration, and the repetitions of "real" (in "really" and "realize") call
into question the very possibility to "know" or "tell" the so-called immigrant experience, the "real" events. Or, as in this passage,

Any family living going on existing is going on and every one can come
to be a dead one and there are then not any more living in that family
living and that family is not then existing if there are not then any more
having come to be living. Any family living is existing if there are some
more being living when very many have come to be dead ones. (925)

Noticeable here are the use of indefinite pronouns (e.g., *any, one, ones,* and
many) and the use of unsettling present participles (e.g., *living, going, existing, having,* and *being*). Instead of nouns that carry with them nominal, isomorphic values crucial in conventional narratives, Stein's pronouns and
participles work consciously to prevent the text from falling back onto
those anchors in narrative. This is primarily to avoid what she has criticized as the "soothing" effect abused in fiction,[32] or what Bernstein has
termed the "artifice of absorption." Such an effect or artifice is one clearly
intended in Kingston's work. For instance, in the opening passage of a
chapter in her *China Men*, "The Making of More Americans," whose title

31. Gertrude Stein, *The Making of Americans: Being a History of a Family's Progress* (1925;
reprint, Normal, Illinois: Daley Archive Press, 1995), 3; emphasis added.
32. Peter Nicholls, *Modernisms: A Literary Guide* (Berkeley and Los Angeles: University of California Press, 1995), 207.

uncannily resonates with Stein's, the prose narrative is smooth and pleasing to an English ear:

> To visit grandfathers, we walked over three sets of railroad tracks, then on sidewalks cracked by grass and tree roots, then a gray dirt path. The roadside weeds waved tall overhead, netting the sunlight and wildflowers. I wore important white shoes for walking to the grandfathers' house. (165)

The smoothness of Kingston's sentences results primarily from the use of "correct" grammar whereas the awkwardness of Stein's is symptomatic of her skepticism of the "natural" laws of human language. Indeed, as Marjorie Perloff suggests, grammar is "taken for granted by most writers [including Kingston] who are 'at home' in their own language and hence are likely to pay more attention to image and metaphor, to figures of heightening, embellishment, and transformation"; but in Stein's writing, grammar "becomes a contested site."[33]

I am not passing judgment on the two writers based on some kind of aesthetic standard. Actually, to many readers, aesthetically, Kingston may fare much better than Stein does. What Stein would have dismissed as the soothing or pleasing effect Kingston has consciously worked to achieve by adopting a standardized linguistic practice has made Kingston a writer much preferred to Stein. Even Harold Bloom, who has cried foul over the increasing popularity of multicultural texts, is willing to edit a volume on Asian American women writers that includes Kingston, but he will never regard Stein's avant-gardism as part of his "Western Canon"[34]—a fact that attests again to what both Bernstein and Guillory have acutely observed as

---

33. Marjorie Perloff, *Wittgenstein's Ladder: Poetic Language and the Strangeness of the Ordinary* (Chicago: University of Chicago Press, 1996), 87.

34. See Harold Bloom, ed., *Asian-American Women Writers* (Philadelphia: Chelsea House Publishers, 1997). See also Marjorie Perloff's article, "Visionary Company," *Boston Review* 23.3–4 (1998), in which she responds critically to Bloom's essay mentioned earlier in this chapter, suggesting that Bloom is on one hand disheartened by multiculturalism and on the other incapable of appreciating the literary innovation by writers such as Stein and Pound.

the correlation between the literary ideology promulgated by certain brands of multicultural studies and that of the traditional humanities.

Besides stylistic differences that actually result from literary ideological differences, we may also compare these two writers with respect to another issue important to both of them—the issue of identity. Attempting to "reclaim America," Kingston insists, as noted earlier, on her own identity as an American: "I am an American writer, who, like other American writers, wants to write the great American novel. *The Woman Warrior* is an American book. Yet many reviewers do not see the American-ness of it, nor the fact of my own American-ness" ("Cultural" 57–58). Kingston's insistence on the Americanness of her own work can be understood as a politicized gesture, however, her problematic literary ideology seems to have outweighed the moral or political values of her work, conveyed and interpreted in a transcendent manner. "The tendency of a literary work," writes Walter Benjamin, "can only be politically correct if it is also literarily correct."[35] Despite her alleged "political correctness," Kingston's work becomes literarily problematic in that it is a positivistic approach to an American identity, which in turn may be reclaimed positivistically by means of standardized American-English writing. In contrast, Stein writes in "Identity A Poem": "I am I because my little dog knows me. The figure wanders on alone. . . . I say two dogs but say a dog and a dog."[36] My identity is only a label by which my little dog knows me. But does even the little dog have an identity? I can say "two dogs," and if you think "two dogs" is a common identity attached to the two dogs, I can simply call them "a dog and a dog," thus separating the same but different "a dog." The indeterminacy of identity results from the impossibility of pinning down which one "a dog" refers to.

"Identity A Poem."

---

35. Walter Benjamin, *Reflections*, ed. Peter Demetz, tr. Edmund Jephcott (New York: Schocken Books, 1978), 221.

36. Gertrude Stein, *A Stein Reader*, ed. Ulla E. Dydo (Evanston: Northwestern University Press, 1993), 588–89.

Identity a poem.

If a person's identity may be just a poem that one can write, revise, publish, or burn, what about a poem's identity? A poem is a text and is not a text because a text does not exist by itself in the intertextual world.

Intertextuality, as demonstrated in my reading of Kingston's work, calls into question the identity of a text. And here even some of the current theories on intertextuality are not sufficient to account for the issue at stake. In these theorizations, there is a common approach in which intertexts are subject to the hegemony of a totalizing text. For Michael Riffaterre, for instance,

> The intertext is what provides the foundation of the text's unity and the text's identity.... The relevant significance is pointed to by some one difficulty insoluble at the level of the text itself: the crux indicates what reversal of markers or exclusion of components is needed for *deducing text from intertext*.[37]

Owen Miller argues for an intertextual identity, one that still "involves some notion of a focused text . . . and some notion of ordering or priority which the reader himself establishes in his engagement with that text."[38] Paul Ricoeur, who follows Martin Heidegger's seminal work *Identity and Difference*, holds out for a "dynamic identity" with which one text both differs from and identifies with other texts through the connection and disconnection of type, genre, and history.[39] Apparently, Ricoeur's notion of intertextuality is still in line with the structuralist concept of contextuality, as understood by Riffaterre and Miller. Therefore, despite the presumed indeterminacy often ascribed to intertextuality by structuralists, intertexts are nothing but materials used to build a stable context. And

37. Michael Riffaterre, "The Making of the Text," in *Identity of the Literary Text*, ed. Mario J. Valdés and Owen Miller (Toronto: University of Toronto Press, 1985), 68; emphasis added.

38. Owen Miller, "Intertextual Identity," in *Identity of the Literary Text*, ed. Mario J. Valdés and Owen Miller (Toronto: University of Toronto Press, 1985), 30.

39. Paul Ricoeur, "The Text as Dynamic Identity," in *Identity of the Literary Text*, ed. Mario J. Valdés and Owen Miller (Toronto: University of Toronto Press, 1985), 183.

context works in the way analogous to how metaphor, as is analyzed by Paul de Man, constitutes a totalizing instance.

In her reading of Kingston, Sau-ling Cynthia Wong also uses "intertext" as one of the two key terms in her study; yet, her application is equally structuralist. Intertextuality enables Wong only to discern the subtexts in a work. Some of these subtexts may be determined as appropriate for the central text and some may be considered as inappropriate and therefore discarded. Wong writes,

> The spirit in which I explore intertextuality in this study is
> catholic—I consider a wide range of possible intertexts for the Asian
> American works under consideration—but what interests me first
> and foremost is how mutual allusion, qualification, complication,
> and transmutation can be discovered between texts regarded as
> Asian American, and how a sense of an internally meaningful literary
> tradition may emerge from such an investigation.[40]

In other words, intertextuality works in the same way as the other key term in her study: context. For Wong, the reader, who in her terms should be a professional critic, can "determine appropriate intertexts" for the text according to the theme (9–10). Thus, what she proposes is in fact a stable hermeneutic structure in which the interpretive subject has absolute control over the interpreted object. And intertextuality is merely a terminological substitute for "interconnection," a structuralist concept that describes the relationship among different parts of a closed structure.

The model of intertextuality I have proposed by means of my critique of Kingston is one that works to the effect of detotalization rather than totalization. In *Allegories of Reading*, Paul de Man suggests that metaphorical systems are totalities because the positing of resemblance between the poles of exchange erases their difference and thus raises them to the status of exchangeable parts of a whole.[41] Instead of

40. Sau-ling Cynthia Wong, *Reading*, 11.
41. See Rodolphe Gasché, *The Wildcard of Reading: On Paul de Man* (Cambridge: Harvard University Press, 1998), 22.

metaphor, de Man proposes the rhetorical as the figural potentiality of language that suspends the totalization of a text. The intertextual relations I have so far unfolded are rhetorical in the de Manian sense—that is, each of the intertexts brings with it the peculiarities of the linguistic practice by means of which the intertext is produced, and the intertexts on which a text is based can never come together as an organic whole. In Kingston's work, however, one major intertext, a prose narrative written in standardized English, is made to appropriate other minor intertexts, in this case "Chinese" legends, myths, and history. The differences among these intertexts, as demonstrated by different linguistic markers, are eradicated in order to create a unitary text. The translation becomes transparent partly because of this operation and partly because it is simply unacknowledged. The ethnography becomes hermeneutic since the representation is left to the narrator, who seldom imagines language itself in the process of imagining the world; the text becomes self-identical since the constituting intertexts are stripped of their differences.

In this way Kingston enters the general assembly of Great American Writers. What she has in her hand is not the sword of a woman warrior, but page after page of Chinese intertexts that have been rewritten in standardized American English, and "bizarre" life stories that are stripped of their linguistic foreignness. Hence her claim: "I'm not even saying that those are Chinese myths anymore. I'm saying I've written down American myths. Fa Mulan and the writing on her back is an American myth. And I made it that way." But somewhere Fa Mulan and Yue Fei are fighting an impossible war, impossible because it has never been allowed to take place in the intertextual world Kingston presents us. But it will be a war nonetheless when linguistic positivism no longer holds readers in its sway or leads them to seek an ethnic experience expressed in a transparent language. When the spell is gone, the intertexts will be like the little ghosts in Kingston's books—running wild, gabbling in their own tongues, and ripping the texts apart.

. . .

As I was writing this chapter, a few weeks after the release of the Disney film *Mulan*, ABC telecast a special program entitled "The Reflection on Ice," starring Olympic silver medalist Michelle Kwan as Mulan. The program—flanked and permeated by the advertisement of McDonald's, which is opening more and more branches in Asia—was a restaging of the film plot, alternating between clips and dramatic performances by the figure skaters. It also included several interviews, one of which was with Ming-na Wen, the voice actor for Mulan in the film. Wen, who also played June in *The Joy Luck Club*, succinctly captured the new "American" spirit that had just been incarnated in the character of Mulan, a spirit the young woman in the thousand-year-old Chinese ballad could never, according to Chin, have been imagined to embody: "She is a role model of individual success." Thus, the journey of Mulan's transpacific migration that leads to her ultimate Americanization is now complete.

SIX

Translation as Ethnography

Problems in American Translations of Contemporary Chinese Poetry

> In order to get clear about aesthetic words, you have
> to describe ways of living.
>
> *Ludwig Wittgenstein*, Lectures and
> Conversations on Aesthetics,
> Psychology, and Religious Belief

And Wittgenstein was right. As Marjorie Perloff shows us in her beautiful study, *Wittgenstein's Ladder* (1996), this exiled philosopher, writing and teaching in a country and language not his own, was keenly aware that "words like 'good' and 'beautiful' have no intrinsic meaning, and that, on the contrary, what matters is the 'occasion' on which these words are said, the uses to which they are put."[1] Therefore, not only is some understanding of ways of living a prerequisite for appreciating aesthetic words, but also aesthetic words are deeply entangled with descriptions of cultural reality—a point I have been arguing throughout my study. And this inseparability between aesthetics and ethnography is borne out again by

1. Marjorie Perloff, *Wittgenstein's Ladder: Poetic Language and the Strangeness of the Ordinary* (Chicago: University of Chicago Press, 1996), 51.

literary translation. Generally speaking, literary translation involves rendering aesthetic or cognitive concepts specific to one linguistic culture into their approximations specific to another culture. In the case of American translations of contemporary Chinese poetry, a topic to which I turn in this chapter, interlingual transpositions are bound to ethnographic descriptions in a problematic manner that bears study.

In his controversial essay "What Is World Poetry?" the eminent Sinologist Stephen Owen accuses contemporary Chinese poetry, such as Bei Dao's, of being too "translatable." He praises Bonnie S. McDougall as a competent translator of Bei Dao's work, and then, based on a somewhat impressionistic evaluation of the translation, he comes to a stunning conclusion:

> We must wonder if such collections of poetry in translation become publishable only because the publisher and the readership have been assured that the poetry was lost in translation. But what if the poetry wasn't lost in translation? What if this is it? This is it.[2]

Such a shocking statement is of course scandalous. And as befits a scandal, it drew angry responses from critics who have vested interests in the politics of contemporary Chinese poetry. Rey Chow, in particular, opens her book *Writing Diaspora* with a critique of what she calls the Orientalist aestheticism at work in Owen's "misreading." Quoting Michelle Yeh, Chow accuses Owen of failing to contextualize Chinese poetry:

> On the one hand, he is disappointed at the lack of history and culture that would distinguish China from other countries. On the other hand, the historical context essential to the writing and reading of contemporary Chinese poetry is not taken seriously and is used only as an occasion for chastising the poet who writes "for self-interest."[3]

But what is this "context" that seems essential to Chow and Yeh? The context, I suppose, is an assumed political reality that often frames the

2. Stephen Owen, "What Is World Poetry?" *New Republic* (November 19, 1990): 31.
3. Rey Chow, *Writing Diaspora: Tactics of Intervention in Contemporary Cultural Studies* (Bloomington: Indiana University Press, 1993), 2.

reading and promotion of a particular kind of contemporary Chinese poetry in the United States. It seems that what is scandalous about Owen's statement is not what Chow has claimed to be his disregard for the context of Chinese poetry. On the contrary, what makes Owen an easy target in the polemic is his expressed skepticism over the preference of political rhetoric to aesthetic values, a preference that is predominant in the reading of contemporary Chinese poetry. Indeed, when treated thematically, much of what has been available in English translation of contemporary Chinese poetry often yields the expected content, familiar in political science and in self-serving U.S. narratives of what it is like to suffer under nondemocratic regimes. Typically, the poems that are introduced tell the story of fighting for democracy, yearning for freedom, awakening to self-consciousness, and rediscovering subjectivity. In other words, these are poems that may easily be contextualized with respect to an image of contemporary China familiar to U.S. readers. It should then become evident that such contextualization, which Chow has criticized Owen for not doing, is a typical ethnographic strategy, textualizing a Chinese reality—which is exactly what Chow has accused Owen of doing (the former is disappointed, in Chow's and Yeh's words, "at the lack of history and culture that would distinguish China from other countries").

Here a dilemma arises: on the one hand, Owen has concluded emphatically that there is really nothing interesting in the translation and that there is really nothing lost in translation—we are stuck with "bad" poetry, and "this is it"; on the other hand, Owen's opponents insist that the poetry be appreciated in its context, but the problematically self-serving contextualization reduces the possibility for the poetry to make its own claims—a point I turn to presently—and therefore it will only further justify Owen's conclusion. The way out of this predicament, I suggest, is to look at an issue that has not been dealt with sufficiently by either side: the issue of translation. It is no wonder that Owen should come to the stunning conclusion that he does, because he regards translation as if it were transparent—McDougall's translation is almost the same as Bei Dao's poems in Chinese ("this is it"). Similarly, in their thematic treatment of Chinese poetry, Chow and others also sidestep the difficulty of translation by advocating a contextualized reading. This, coming from Chow, who seems to have written in a well-informed manner about translation in her recent work, may look like a surprise; but it hardly is. When it comes to the issue of translation, whether in the case of Chinese poetry or Chinese cinema, Chow's discussion often remains confined to the realm of thematization.[4] In spite of the significance of contextuality, such reading often fails to recognize the problems in translation caused by textuality itself, textuality that lies at the heart of the Chinese poets' experimentation.[5] As I demonstrate in the following case

4. For instance, in the final section of her study of Chinese cinema, *Primitive Passions: Visuality, Sexuality, Ethnography, and Contemporary Chinese Cinema* (New York: Columbia University Press, 1995), Chow deals with the issue of translation, maintaining that the films she has discussed should be understood as ethnographies, or cultural translations. While Chow's entire book claims to deal with visuality but actually pays little attention to visuality as produced in the technical process of filmmaking (visuality to Chow is almost never an embodiment of opaque materiality but always a transparent sign to be interpreted), this last section, entitled "Film as Ethnography; or, Translation between Cultures in the Postcolonial World," is primarily a discussion of some key texts on translation (Benjamin, de Man, Derrida, etc.). What Chow fails to answer, however, are questions of how translation works on the technical or formal level—which, just like the formal dimension of Chinese poetry, is profoundly cultural and political but cannot be grasped thematically. Take for instance the following passage from the section: "Contemporary Chinese films are cultural 'translations' in these multiple senses of the term. By consciously exoticizing China and revealing China's 'dirty secrets' to the outside world, contemporary Chinese directors are translators of the violence with which the Chinese culture is 'originally' put together. In the dazzling colors of their screen, the primitive that is woman, who at once unveils the corrupt Chinese tradition and parodies the orientalism of the West, stands as the naive symbol, the brilliant arcade, through which 'China' travels across cultures to unfamiliar audiences" (202).

Here, except for the impressionistic mentioning of "the dazzling bright colors of the screens," words and phrases such as *exoticizing, dirty secrets, violence, primitive, woman, symbol, arcade,* and *unfamiliar,* significantly loaded terms as they are, reveal the schematic character of Chow's interpretation—that is, these are not terms used to mark the visual or textual differences and to register the complexity of intersemiotic transpositions, both of which are issues at stake in translation.

5. If my critique of Chow and others sounds strong, it is only because of the urgency I feel to raise the issue at stake. And I do so out of great respect for Chow and others as

studies, the so-called contextualized reading often skews the translation of a Chinese poem toward a version that may easily yield a theme compatible with the preconceived "context" or ethnographicized "reality."

Translation is a site for negotiation between the text and the translator about poetics, ideology, and history. In the case of American translations of contemporary Chinese poetry, such negotiation takes place between the irreducible formal—and by no means less social—materiality embodied by the text and the simplistic ideological reduction practiced by the translator. The outcome, as seen in the currently available translations, is an intertextual transformation, a process that is thoroughly ethnographic. Yet, it is ethnography not only in the Wittgensteinian sense, that aesthetic words are intertwined with cultural descriptions, that "to imagine a language means to imagine a form of life"; it is also understood in the way I have argued throughout this book—that ethnography relies on intertextual tactics of absorbing texts, transforming them into "ideal" versions, capturing key words, inserting interpretations, and ultimately, making the translation appear transparent, making the translator's intervening hand disappear into invisibility.

The U.S. translation and promotion of contemporary Chinese poetry, which have focused primarily on the post–Cultural Revolution period, starts with Stephen C. Soong and John Minford's *Trees on the Mountain* (1984). Since then, major anthologies include Edward Morin's *The Red Azalea* (1990), Donald Finkel and Carolyn Kizer's *A Splintered Mirror* (1991), Michelle Yeh's *Anthology of Modern Chinese Poetry* (1992), Tony Barnstone's *Out of the Howling Storm* (1993), and Ping Wang's *New Generation* (1999). Major collections of the works of individual poets include

---

cultural critics. However, if the authors I criticize really mean well for contemporary Chinese poetry (or, for that matter, transpacific studies), then I especially feel the need to call attention to the fact that the desire for a "politically correct" reading of Chinese poetry is paradoxically doing a great disservice to the poetic works, a fact that many Chinese poets, with whom I have corresponded, have sadly acknowledged.

Bei Dao's *Notes from the City of the Sun, August Sleepwalker, Old Snow, Forms of Distance,* and *Landscape over Zero;* Gu Cheng's *Selected Poems;* Yang Lian's *Masks and Crocodile;* and Duo Duo's *Looking Out from Death.*[6] Predominantly represented in these translation works is the Misty School, led by the "Today" group: Bei Dao, Duo Duo, Gu Cheng, Yang Lian, Shu Ting, and Man Ke. These poets are well known for their prodemocratic political stance, and their poems often articulate a yearning for freedom and individuality. However, the political themes of their poetry are expressed in forms far more complex than the American translators have presented.

Here is a poem by Bei Dao, translated by David Hinton:

PLAYWRIGHT

in the moon's morning of postpartum convalescence
a chair's stationed on the railway platform
the train's mute departure
zips open that secret landscape
where music thundered down a skyful of snow
and flames in the stables venture forth
direction signs awaken one-by-one
night and day diverging where the routes fork
destination: a room booked ahead

he opens doors of double-identity onto a balcony
and introduces smoke to clear blue skies
those scarecrows drenched after heavy rains[7]

Regardless of the theme of this poem, one thing should be clear: There is a change of scene from night to day, from dark to light. This change is represented in the translated version by "the moon" in the beginning

---

6. I have included on this list some publications that did not appear in the United States but rather in other English-speaking countries. However, many of these publications have been promoted and read in the same problematic way that I am describing here.

7. Bei Dao, *Forms of Distance,* trans. David Hinton (New York: New Directions, 1994), 23.

versus "clear blue skies" in the end; "signs awaken"; and "night and day diverging." Yet, the semantic flow in the translation is nowhere comparable to the formal experimentation in the original poem. The Chinese for "railway platform" in the second line is *yue tai*, literally meaning, "moon stage"; and the Chinese for "balcony" in the first line of the second stanza is *yang tai*, literally "sun stage." Also, "clear blue skies" after "balcony" translates *qing kong*, literally "sunny skies." Therefore, the formal structure of the original poem can be outlined as:

moon
    moon stage
(night and day diverging)
    sun stage
sunny skies

It should be obvious that the inner syntax constructed by the Chinese characters and by the resonances and reverberations between key words in the original has been eliminated through the translator's semantic rendering.[8]

It is true that a text is always subject to different readings, and in translation the leeway for differences is even wider. It might seem that, taking into account the linguistic difference between alphabetic English and ideographic Chinese, the problem with Hinton's version is only a matter of stylistic preference. But that is hardly the case. When I contacted the Chinese consultant who had helped Hinton with the translation of Bei Dao's poems,[9] I suggested the possibility of using annotation to give English readers some idea about the formal experimentation in "Playwright." The reply was, "We believe that there shouldn't be any

8. See my book *Shi: A Radical Reading of Chinese Poetry* (New York: Roof Books, 1997), in which I also argue for a reading that takes the formal and conceptual dimensions of Chinese poetry into full account.

9. It is still a common practice in American translations of contemporary Chinese poetry that the translator, who knows some but not enough Chinese, collaborates with a native Chinese speaker—a practice reminiscent of a fieldwork situation in anthropology, where the ethnographer uses a native interpreter.

notes in poetry," meaning that footnotes or endnotes would only trivialize the significance of the poem and thereby contaminate its purity. This ideal of purity, as Lawrence Venuti argues, implies a will to fluent, transparent translation:

> A translated text . . . is judged acceptable by most publishers, reviewers, and readers when it reads fluently, when the absence of any linguistic or stylistic peculiarities makes it seem transparent. . . . The illusion of transparency is an effect of fluent discourse, of the translator's effort to insure easy readability by adhering to current usage, maintaining continuous syntax, fixing a precise meaning. What is so remarkable here is that this illusory effect conceals the numerous conditions under which the translation is made, starting with the translator's crucial intervention in the foreign text.[10]

For Venuti, the unwillingness to provide annotation for foreign poems indicates the translator's effort to make the reader believe that the translation is the original—or, as Owen puts it, "This is it." But in fact, as in "Playwright," while the translation seems as neat and fluent as an original, the significant formal (and perhaps even foreign) experimentation of the poet is elided without acknowledgment. The translator's intervening hand becomes invisible, thus justifying Owen's lament that the poetry is too "translatable."[11]

Another example in which linguistic peculiarities are elided for the sake of fluent and transparent translation can be found in Tony Barnstone's rendering of Shu Ting's "Assembly Line." The first stanza reads:

Night after night,
the assembly line of time.

10. Lawrence Venuti, *The Translator's Invisibility: A History of Translation* (New York: Routledge, 1995), 1–2.

11. Owen's equating of the translation with the original is predicated on a belief that contemporary Chinese poetry has been so deeply influenced by Western literatures that it reads almost the same as the latter and therefore nothing is lost in translation. Yet, as I argue in this chapter, translation still has played an indispensable role in the literary interaction and cultural description.

After work at the factory's assembly line
we join the homebound lines
as stars above assemble to cross the sky.
Over there
a line of lost saplings.[12]

But a literal translation runs in this way:

In the assembly line of time
night and night lie closely together
we withdraw from the factory's assembly line
again teaming in a homebound assembly line
above us the stars' assembly line crossing the sky
beside us
young trees are lost on an assembly line

Barnstone's translation does have its beauty and simplicity; but compared with the literal one, it is noticeable that the translation is different in several ways: (1) the addition of punctuation marks; (2) the reduction of the repetition of "assembly line" to "line," in part of the stanza; (3) the elimination of the original parallel structure of "over us ... / beside us ..."; and (4) the rewording of the first two lines.

Adding punctuation does make the poem easier to read, partly because punctuation, as Venuti puts it, "fix[es] a precise meaning." But in this case punctuation eliminates the sense of floating—as on an assembly line—produced in the original. Likewise, the five repetitions of "assembly line" in the original may sound excessive to the translator, but they evoke the dullness of a worker's life in a state-owned factory, an effect I believe the poem intends to create. The parallel structure also adds to the sense of repetition, but the translator introduces a more varied pattern. The refusal to stay with a literal rendering of the first two lines is probably attributable to the same factor—the translator's desire for a version that is clean in form and clear in content.

12. Tony Barnstone, ed., *Out of the Howling Storm: The New Chinese Poetry* (Middletown, Conn.: Wesleyan University Press, 1993), 60.

Changes such as these are often characterized as stylistic variations. But, as I have argued in the cases of Imagism, Kingston, and others, style is too light a word to describe a crucial intertextual strategy adopted in translation and ethnography. In the present case, the changes reduce the formal experimentation in the original to a minimal level, creating a different aesthetics that might be more familiar to English readers of the kind who find the neat images in the poems of Robert Frost, Robert Bly, or James Wright appealing. More important still, the formal reduction is intimately tied to an ideological reduction and ethnographic essentialization: It reduces Chinese poetry to expressions of a few political themes rendered in precise imagery and makes the translation itself into an ethnographic account of the political reality of contemporary China.

Such twinning of intertextual transformation and ethnographic essentialization is evident in the handling of "A Day," another poem by Bei Dao. The earliest translation by Bonnie S. McDougall runs like this:

To lock my secrets in a drawer
leave notes in the margin of a favorite book
put a letter in the postbox and stand in silence for a while
sizing up passers-by in the wind, without misgivings
studying the shop windows' flashing neon lights
to drop in a coin in the telephone booth
ask a cigarette from the old fellow fishing under the bridge
while the river steamer sounds its huge vast siren
to stare at myself through clouds of smoke
in the dim full-length mirror in the theatre lobby
and when the curtain closes off the clamor of the sea of stars
leaf through faded photos and old letters in the lamplight[13]

A new version of McDougall's translation appears in Barnstone's anthology, and it changes some crucial words: the pronouns. The first line becomes "Lock up your secrets with a drawer"; the ninth line runs

13. Bei Dao, *Notes from the City of the Sun*, ed. and trans. Bonnie S. McDougall (Ithaca: China-Japan Program, Cornell University, 1984), 35.

"stare at yourself through clouds of smoke." The only two pronouns in the original can be literally translated as "one's" *(zijide)*, and "oneself" *(ziji)*. They could refer to the poet himself ("I"), the reader ("you"), or a third person ("he" or "she"). In fact, there could be more than one person involved; each act in the poem could be accomplished by a different person and each perspective attributed to a different person. As Bei Dao states clearly in his essay "About Poetry": "I try to introduce in my own poetry the technique of film montage, and by creating juxtaposed images and changes in speed, I want to arouse people's imaginations to fill in the substantial gaps between the words" (*Notes* 79).

Taking Bei Dao's artistic goal into consideration, the best rendering of the pronouns in "A Day" seems to be the indefinite "one," which may help to create a sense of "juxtaposed images" viewed possibly from different perspectives. The changes in McDougall's new version from "my" to "your" and from "myself" to "yourself" indicate at least the translator's awareness of the formal significance of the pronouns.

By contrast, in the introduction to her *Anthology of Modern Chinese Poetry*, the editor and translator Michelle Yeh renders part of "A Day" as follows:

> I gaze at myself through the smoke
> In the dim mirror at the theater entrance.
> When curtains block off the noise of the sea of stars,
> I open the faded album and read the traces of words. (xxxii)

The added punctuation, which is intended, as Yeh claims, to "aid readability," actually does a disservice to Bei Dao's idea of juxtaposing images. Moreover, Yeh inserts first-person pronouns that did not exist in the original. The apparent explanation of this insertion can be found in what Yeh states immediately before and after those four quoted lines:

> Inseparable from the issue of style was the issue of content. What the [Communist] establishment probably found most unacceptable [in Misty Poetry] was the emphasis on individualism and self-expression.... His "Days" [i.e., "A Day"] suggests the return of

the individual by adopting an unmistakably personal perspective.... Self-perception and self-reflexivity surface in the two concluding images.... From the murky fog and the darkness of the night emerges a self, solitary yet self-contained, with a rich world of memories and imagination. (xxxii)

To the translator, the thematic reading of the poem as an expression of individualism under the oppression of a Communist regime calls for the insertion of a subjective "I." The result is both a clichéd version of Bei Dao's poetry as the poetry of self-expression and a familiar account of contemporary China.

In the United States of the past few decades, from TVs to newspapers, magazines, films, popular fiction / nonfiction, school lectures, and institutional researches, the everyday story about China is not very different from this: A totalitarian regime oppresses millions of people who fight for individual freedom and self-expression. A quick glance at some of the book titles, prefaces, and journal editorials suffices to demonstrate how the poetry translations have contributed to the production of such an ethnographic image, a process quite reminiscent of Imagism. Here are two book titles: *A Splintered Mirror: Chinese Poetry from the Democracy Movement* and *The Red Azalea: Chinese Poetry since the Cultural Revolution*. An editorial in *Prairie Schooner* states:

> Now, as this special issue [of Chinese literature] goes to press...
> Liu Xiaobo, a Chinese scholar who helped lead the hunger strike in
> Tiananmen Square, is being tried for political dissent behind closed
> doors in Beijing—along with twenty-four participants in the failed
> democracy movement.[14]

David Hinton writes in the introduction to his book of translation of Bei Dao's poems: "Bei Dao's very different cultural context allowed him to use surrealist techniques for his own unique purposes. The

14. Hilda Raz, editorial, *Prairie Schooner* 65. 2 (1991): 4.

more private and introspective his work became, the more subversively political it was."[15]

In all of these cases Chinese poetry is contextualized against its political background—the democracy movement. Even Rey Chow, as sophisticated a critic as she is, often relies on an ethnographically essentialized image of mainland China for her articulations of diasporic thinking.[16] In her *Writing Diaspora*, for instance, she describes the contemporary historical context in a manner that even she herself has characterized as "schematic":

> And even though the Chinese Communists once served as the anti-
> imperialist inspiration for other "third world" cultures and progres-
> sive Western intellectuals, that dream of a successful and consistent
> opposition to the West on ideological grounds has been dealt the
> death blow by more recent events such as the Tiananmen Square
> Massacre of 1989, in which the Chinese government itself acted as
> viciously as if it were one of its capitalist enemies. As the champion
> of the unprivileged classes and nations of the world, Communist
> China has shown itself to be a failure, a failure which is now hanging
> on by empty official rhetoric while its people choose to live in ways
> that have obviously departed from the Communist ideal. (8–9)

My point is not to dispute the historical facts as such, but rather to identify a problematic model of literary studies, a model that Stephen Greenblatt, as noted earlier, has called "a priori ideological determinism." I describe the possible pitfall of this model of contextualization, because it is, paradoxically, doing serious historical damage to Chinese poetry. Not only have the artistic goals of the poets not been taken seri-

---

15. Bei Dao, *Forms*, vii.

16. See my article "Writing against the Chinese Diaspora" (*boundary 2: An International Journal of Literature and Culture* 26.1 [1999]: 145–46) in which I suggest that much of current writing about the Chinese diaspora is predicated on the idea of a preexisting homogeneous mainland China. What is interesting in these writings, I argue, is not how people live diasporically, but how they imagine themselves living diasporically, or how the homogeneity, to which the diaspora is fashioned as the antithesis, has been imagined.

ously by the critics, but the kind of contextualization the latter practice often works against the literary ideology of the former. The notion that literature should clearly express political messages has been promoted and abused by the Communist establishment for a long time. It was against this positivistic and utilitarian literary ideology that the Misty School led a new poetry movement in China, and it is certainly ironic that, in the United States today, the same literary ideology has accompanied the interpretation and translation of this school's poetry. It is no wonder that Shu Ting shook her head again and again at a poetry reading entitled "A Splintered Mirror"[17] in San Francisco, May 1992; and it is no wonder that Bei Dao lamented at a poetry conference held at Cornell University, April 1994: "Americans don't read our poetry."

In response to such reductive approaches to contemporary Chinese poetry, there should not only be a call for a re-reading of the poetry of Bei Dao's generation, which still dominates the stage of representation in the United States, but also a different way of reading and translating the "new poetry" that comes after the Misty School. Among the few translations that focus on the new poetry, two projects have distinguished themselves: Ping Wang's *New Generation: Poems from China Today* and Jeffrey Twitchell's introduction of the "Original" group.

A bilingual poet and fiction writer herself, Ping Wang presents the English-speaking world with the most comprehensive picture to date of the recent experimentation in Chinese poetry. Her anthology includes about two dozen post-Misty poets: Chen Dongdong, Liang Xiaoming, Liu Manliu, Meng Lang, Mo Fei, Mo Mo, Wang Jiaxin, Xi Chuan, Xue Di, Yan Li, Zai Yoming, Zhang Zhen, Zhao Qiong, Zhen Danyi, Zou Jingzi, and others. Her introduction provides a contextualized discussion of the thematic dimension of the poems. But her contextualization, unlike the ones discussed earlier, is not done with lack of attention to the

17. This is a reference to Donald Finkel and Carolyn Kizer's thematically organized anthology, *A Splintered Mirror: Chinese Poetry from the Democracy Movement* (San Francisco: North Point Press, 1991).

formal materiality of the poetry, and her thematic reading never results simply in a few extralinguistic "-isms." For instance, when she situates the new poetry in the atmosphere of globalization and national transformation, she attends closely to the poem's linguistic peculiarity:

> Many of the "new generation" poets tend to subject time to the service of space, and project the transformation of social relations, political institutions, and cultural differences onto the vision of place and landscape. . . . Yu Jian exhibits a unique form of spatial exploration through a block-like physical presence. In his poems, punctuation is completely eliminated. This seems to be a restoration of Chinese traditional writing which required no punctuation. But Yu Jian makes a difference by inserting physical spaces between words and sentences to replace commas and periods, the signs for duration stops (signs for time). The blank spaces take as important a position in his poems as the words do. They function as a background for the contents, a negative for the paintings. Furthermore, Yu Jian drops the traditional poetic forms of the line breaks and stanzas. His poems are nothing but large blocks of texts composed of heaps of fragments and objects.[18]

Such close attention to the linguistic peculiarity is materialized in the process of her translation. Yu Jian's poem appears as "huge blocks" and "heaps of fragments and objects":

> Everything is the same   space   color   voice   texture
>   weight and heart
> the chandelier above   the floor below   the left hand on
>   the left   the right hand on the right
> the bed in the corner   near the window   next to the
>   dresser and mirror
> the trunk on top   the shoes at the bottom   the food

---

18. I am quoting from an earlier manuscript version of Ping Wang's introduction, which is different from the one published in the book, pp. 21–22.

in the cabinet
The left hand can reach aspirin and thermos
    glass and cigarettes
The right hand can get oranges   box of candy   magazines
    a bit farther there are matches
Half a step forward   I can touch the sofa   it sinks as I sit[19]

Wang's idea of translation is not beyond question. When she writes, "I finally gave up the impossible task of finding the exact equivalence in English to replace the original, and let the foreign tongue penetrate and grasp the essential intention of the original" (30), there still exists the unwillingness to allow the real foreign—Chinese—to enter into the closed sophistication of English poetic diction. However, her translation as an introduction of the new Chinese poetry is in some respects a groundbreaking work. Her emphasis on the formal materiality of the poetry, as opposed to reductive thematic treatments, will lead us to the threshold of new practices of translating Chinese poetry.

In this respect, Jeffrey Twitchell's unceasing efforts in translating and introducing the Original poets provide the best example of a sincere commitment to reading Chinese poetry and to opening up the potentialities of English. A Ph.D. graduate from Duke University, Twitchell went to teach in Nanjing, a Chinese city not far from where the Original group is based. This poetry group belongs to the so-called Third or New Generation and includes Che Qianzi, Zhou Yaping, Huang Fan, Yi Chun, and Hong Liu. Their poetics is best represented in their "Manifesto of Spring 1988":

When the poet's consciousness shifts to language, this is in fact the preparatory stage of modern artistic experiment. We think the first step of such experiment is: the written characters alone (the code of recording language) is the starting point, only in this way will the

19. Ping Wang, *The New Generation: Poems from China Today* (New York: Hanging Loose Press, 1999), 181.

exploration of human spiritual phenomena and especially of individual phenomena be possible.[20]

Such a recognition of language as the "house of Being" demands a translation that does not create mere thematic reduction, but rather foregrounds the differences between the languages; that does not try to conceal itself, but rather is self-conscious of its intertextual nature.

From this point of view, Twitchell's treatment of one of the most exciting experiments in Chinese poetry is superb. His attentive reading of the linguistic peculiarities of both Chinese and English and his painstaking efforts in constructing English poetic artifice as an intertextual dialogue with the Chinese poems are exemplified in his translation of "An Incident: The Supper," by Che Qianzi:

> Red kid, father, grandmother. Congee being ladled into bowls.
>> Paper-thin congee
> Flowing into rough bowls
> A necessary game for labor and growing up
> For hunger, this is the reward
> Simple, reverent and full of gratitude
> No sound is uttered, heads in eating bowls / evening bell is
>> ringing on the farm / no word
> Is spoken[21]

With the assistance from the poet himself, Twitchell provides detailed annotation for these lines:

> 1. The phrase we have here translated as "red kid" is more literally "naked kid" and idiomatically suggests an innocent. Che Qianzi notes that this phrase is meant to include the meanings "little rascal," "newborn babe," and "little red guard."

20. Jeffrey Twitchell, "Original: Chinese Language-Poetry Group," in *Exact Change Yearbook* no. 1 (Boston: Exact Change, 1995), 36.

21. Jeffrey Twitchell, "Chinese Poetic Postmodernism? Introduction to the Original Poets," *Polygraph* 5 (1992): 228.

2. In the best sense of a farm with reverence, there is no concept of "farm" here.

3. There is no evening bell on the farm. "Evening bell" is pronounced the same as "in the bowl." (Ibid. 229)

These notes make the translator conspicuously visible since they make the reader aware of the formal construction created by the translator himself. In the line "No sound is uttered, heads in eating bowls / evening bell is," the notes explain that the word *eating* has been added by the translator to replace *the*. This addition can in no way be compared to the insertion of an ideological *I* in Yeh's case. Instead, it is a construct added by the translator to achieve some formal effects: "eating bowls / evening bell is" alliterates /b/ and /ls/ and rhymes /ing/, let alone the visual similarity between the shapes of the two phrases. The replacement of *the* by *eating* does not simply make the translation formally parallel the original as closely as possible; more important, it demonstrates the translator's commitment to the formal materiality of poetic language and to the poetics espoused by the Original poets: form is meaning.

Yet, the question remains as to what to make of Twitchell's work in light of my earlier claim that textual translation is irrevocably cultural translation, or simply, ethnography. Before I answer this question, a better understanding of the nature of ethnography is necessary. Throughout this book, I have differentiated two conceptions of ethnography: one regards ethnography as a social science–based work, proclaiming the ethnographer's ability to capture the essence of a culture in a scientific, objective manner; the other recognizes the textual and intertextual nature of ethnography, foregrounding ethnographic work's linguisticality and discursivity. I have also explained the difference between these two radically opposing conceptions of ethnography from the perspectives of poetics and hermeneutics. In terms of poetics, they draw upon different economies of meaning: one upon the utilitarian and positivistic function of language and the other upon the mediated and ruptured function of language. In terms of hermeneutics, they represent different interpretive models: one highlights the split between interpreting subjectivity and interpreted objectivity, and the other recognizes the impossibility of the split and stresses the ontological nature of understanding mediated by language.

From this perspective, Twitchell's work is ethnography, but it surely is an ethnography that questions the very possibility of ethnography. This is very clear from his attempts to eradicate the illusion of transparency in translation by providing elaborate annotation that undercuts the authority of his English version. Twitchell's self-undercutting should be understood as a gesture of self-marking/mocking, a gesture suggesting that his English version is only a result of intertextual transformation, rather than an exact, transparent equivalence. Indeed, both Twitchell's self-marking/mocking and the thematic reduction in the case of Yeh and other translators mentioned earlier constitute ethnography, but they represent very different approaches to contemporary Chinese poetry and have very different implications for transpacific cultural poetics and politics.

Much progress has occurred since the time when many Chinese poems first appeared on mimeographed sheets of the worst-quality paper. Now they appear in well-printed, perfectly bound English anthologies. But there is still a long way to go in terms of representing contemporary Chinese poetry to English-language readers. The task of translation is even more demanding when there are still numerous examples of translated works that may justify Owen's conclusion, and especially when Chinese poetry continues to be read by Owen's critics as confirmation of their own ethnographic description of China. By critiquing the ethnographic strategies used to thematize Chinese poetry, I not only question the politics embedded in a certain kind of contextualization but also call for a reading that is not simply a self-verification of some crude political interest, but one that is fully committed to the inseparable formal and social materiality of the poetry. Such commitment cannot be realized in transparent translations or in reductive thematizations. Instead, it is to be found in practices that set out to question the very possibility of translation and to recognize fully the intertextual, intercultural nature of transpacific displacement.

Conclusion

What I have described as transpacific displacement is a historical process of dislocation and relocation of cultural meanings via ethnography, translation, and intertextual travel. Interestingly, this complicated cross-over, of which Imagism's appropriation and reinvention of "Chinese" poetics constitute an important part, now seems to have taken an unexpected turn: readers of contemporary Chinese poetry have been told that the work in front of them is influenced, inspired by Imagism. As the story goes, Chinese poets, such as Bei Dao and Gu Cheng, living in the poetic wasteland of the Cultural Revolution, turned to Western literature for inspiration. The books circulated clandestinely among the underground reading-club members (consisting mainly of young rebellious writers) included those by Tolstoy, Turgenev, Kafka, Baudelaire, and Pound. In the case of Pound, especially, his use of Chinese characters enabled the young poets to recognize the values of classical Chinese poetry, which had been banished by the Chinese Communist literary orthodoxy, and helped to justify their efforts to recuperate those values by means of their own new poetic creations—they started to appropriate Pound and the other Imagists! If such an account is historically accurate, then we are indeed witnessing a twisted, reversed trajectory of transpacific displacement. We may even be tempted to say that this reversal has brought the process of intertextual migration to a full circle.[1]

But a circle is a closed, insulated trajectory, opposite to the ones I have described, which crisscross, parallel, repeat, or even trample one another. While the implications this particular reversal may have for "Chinese" literature remain a topic to be addressed elsewhere, the possibility that cultural meanings migrate and then return by intertextual means under specific historical circumstances should no longer be considered an anomaly in literary history by those who have accompanied me thus far in this book. Throughout this volume, I have tried to demonstrate in the most concrete terms textual migrations across the Pacific; and even though I have focused mainly on American appropriations of Asian poetics rather than the opposite, there should be no doubt that transpacific displacement is not and can never be one-way traffic.

To delineate the multirouted, multidirectional trajectories across the Pacific is not, however, the ultimate goal of my project. What most concerns me is how the rediscovery of these textual trajectories may lead to our reconception of "American" literature. In the recent decades, both the New Americanists and Asian Americanists have contributed greatly to the expansion of the American literary canon.[2] As has been demonstrated especially in the work of the latter, the new focus on the Pacific has generated a critical discourse that ineluctably transgresses the old cultural and geographical boundaries of "America." My book is intended to complement these approaches, to make a modest contribution to the exploration of new boundaries of American literature and to the reimagining of a

1. For a well-informed and insightful discussion of this issue, see Xiaomei Chen, *Occidentalism: A Theory of Counter-Discourse in Post-Mao China* (New York: Oxford University Press, 1995).

2. For the first group, see Philip Fisher, ed., *The New American Studies* (1991); Donald Pease, ed., *National Identities and Post-Americanist Narratives* (1994); Donald Pease, ed., *Revisionary Interventions into the Americanist Canon* (1994); José David Saldívar, *Border Matters: Remapping American Cultural Studies* (1997); John Carlos Rowe, *Literary Culture and U.S. Imperialism* (2000). For the second group, see Arif Dirlik (1993), Lisa Lowe (1996), David Palumbo-Liu (1999), and Rob Wilson (2000).

transpacific, intercultural chronotope. If I could claim any uniqueness for my project, I would make so bold as to assert that it lies in my efforts to unpack the layers and stages of linguistic mediation that are charged with intercultural politics and history but never easily reducible to any single predetermining ideology in the positivistic sense.

My focus on language and textuality derives from my conviction that literature does its cultural work as much through its nontransparent aesthetic form as through its often-transparent thematic content. Two examples from literary history, one classic and the other modern, should suffice to explain what I mean by such a statement. After Plato propagated the ostracism of poets from his Republic, Aristotle wrote *Poetics* in part to defend them. Whereas Plato's accusation was based largely on moral standards extraneous to poetry, Aristotle's defense relied on an understanding of the intrinsic values of poetry in relation to other discourses, such as philosophy and history, and on a reconception of the distinct ways poetry relates to reality. The remarkable clarity and forcefulness of the opening sentence of *Poetics* are quite telling in proportion to what Aristotle sees as the essential values of poetry: "I propose to treat of Poetry in itself and of its various kinds, noting the essential quality of each" (1.1). What Aristotle proposed to do was by no means to ignore the moral issues involved in poetry and treat only poetic, aesthetic forms. Instead, he drew attention to morality embodied, mediated by the making of poetry rather than moral values in any transcendent sense.

Similarly, Walter Benjamin defended art against schematic interpretations that often became tools used in radical politics either to condemn art that was insubordinate to political goals or to strip art of its own critical function. In "The Work of Art in the Age of Mechanical Reproduction," for example, Benjamin discusses the politics of film not in terms of its thematic content but from the perspective of the cultural logic that is embodied in the making of film. In "The Author as Producer," Benjamin goes even further in recognition of the politics of artistic form by asserting that "the concept of political tendency . . . is a perfectly useless instrument of political literary criticism. . . . The tendency of a literary work can only be politically correct if it is also literarily correct."[3] Here Benjamin echoes some of the famous statements made by Aristotle in *Poetics*, such as "The standard of correctness is not the same in poetry and politics, any more than in poetry and any other art," and "Not to know that a hind has no horns is a less serious matter than to paint it inartistically" (25.3; 25.5). What Benjamin means by "literarily correct," or what Aristotle sees as "the standard of correctness," as I take it, pertains to a practice in production or criticism that engages with what makes art art in the first place, that is, the mechanics of artistic creation.[4]

What Aristotle and Benjamin provide for me is a way to locate the ideology and historicity of literary works not merely in their thematic content but also, perhaps even more so, in their aesthetic form. Such an approach to literature is especially pertinent to my project as I demonstrate a making of American literature that is unthinkable without taking into account its intercultural, intertextual appropriations. Transpacific displacement is above all a historical process of textual migration, which involves the attempts made by American writers, ethnographers, and translators to appropriate, capture, mimic, parody, or revise the Other's signifying practices, attempts that in turn lead to changes and developments in American literature. In order to expand the parameters of such a national literature and to explore its international dimensions, it is certainly indispensable to speak of the nation's imperialist past and its effects on the literature we are reading; but it is equally important to take stock of the linguistic appropriations that physically make up the body of the literature. It is especially significant to understand how such "marvelous possessions" may become agents of dispossession, how the appropriations may create an existential dilemma for the appropriators, and how, in other words, literature does its cultural work not only by passively reflecting social reality but also by actively producing and changing reality.

3. Walter Benjamin, *Reflections*, ed. Peter Demetz, trans. Edmund Jephcott (New York: Schocken Books, 1978), 221.

4. I am indebted to Lindsay Waters for the discussion of the link between Benjamin and Aristotle.

If we can recognize clearly the significance of America's transpacific experience and understand fully the extent to which American literature owes its existence to intercultural migrations, the project I just presented to you should have at least three implications. First, there ought to be a reconception of American literature in the context of transnationalism, a rewriting of its history as one rooted in transnationalism and committed to intercultural (transpacific, transatlantic, transcontinental) practices. Second, we need to reconsider American literature in the context of multilingualism, acknowledging that the literature, as we know it, is a body of multilingual writings, consisting not only of works that have been and continue to be written in languages other than English but also of works that are inherently polyglot.[5] Third, we need to reimagine a literature that is no longer confined to national, cultural, or linguistic boundaries, a literature that emerges from and belongs to the transpacific. To bring all these ramifications to fruition will take much more effort, and this book is only the beginning.

5. See Werner Sollors, ed., *Multilingual America: Transnationalism, Ethnicity, and the Languages of American Literature* (New York: New York University Press, 1998); and Werner Sollors and Marc Shell, eds., *Multilingual Anthology of American Literature* (New York: New York University Press, 2000).

BIBLIOGRAPHY

Althusser, Louis. *Lenin and Philosophy and Other Essays*. Trans. Ben Brewster. New York: Monthly Review Press, 1971.

Amirthanayagam, Guy, ed. *Asian and Western Writers in Dialogue: New Cultural Identities*. London: Macmillan, 1982.

Aristotle. *Poetics*. Trans. S. H. Butcher. New York: Hill and Wang, 1961.

Austin, J. L. *How to Do Things with Words*. Oxford: Oxford University Press, 1962.

Austin, Mary. *The American Rhythm: Studies and Reexpressions of Amerindian Songs*. 1923. Reprint, New York: Cooper Square Publishers, 1970.

Ayscough, Florence. *A Chinese Mirror: Being Reflections of the Reality behind Appearances*. Boston: Houghton Mifflin, 1925.

———. *Chinese Women: Yesterday and Today*. Boston: Houghton Mifflin, 1937.

———. *Fir-Flower Tablets: Poems from the Chinese*. Trans. Amy Lowell. Boston: Houghton Mifflin, 1921.

———. *Florence Ayscough and Amy Lowell: Correspondence of a Friendship*. Ed. Harley Farnsworth MacNair. Chicago: University of Chicago Press, 1945.

———. "Proem." In *Within the Walls of Nanking*, by Alice Tisdale Hobart. London: Jonathan Cape, 1928.

———. *Tu Fu: The Biography of a Chinese Poet*. Boston: Houghton Mifflin, 1929.

———. "Written Pictures." *Poetry* 13 (February 1919): 268–72.

Bacon, Francis. *The Advancement of Learning and the New Atlantis*. 1605. Reprint, New York: Oxford University Press, 1951.

Bakhtin, Mikhail. *The Dialogic Imagination: Four Essays*. Ed. Michael Holquist. Trans. Caryl Emerson and Michael Holquist. Austin: University of Texas Press, 1981.

189

———. *Problems of Dostoevsky's Poetics.* Ed. and trans. Caryl Emerson. Minneapolis: University of Minnesota Press, 1984.

Barkan, Elazar, and Ronald Bush, eds. *Prehistories of the Future: The Primitivist Project and the Culture of Modernism.* Stanford: Stanford University Press, 1995.

Barnstone, Tony, ed. *Out of the Howling Storm: The New Chinese Poetry.* Middletown, Conn.: Wesleyan University Press, 1993.

Barthes, Roland. *Empire of Signs.* Trans. Richard Howard. New York: Hill and Wang, 1982.

———. *Image, Music, Text.* Trans. Stephen Heath. New York: Hill and Wang, 1977.

Bei Dao. *The August Sleepwalker.* Trans. Bonnie S. McDougall. New York: New Directions, 1988.

———. *Forms of Distance.* Trans. David Hinton. New York: New Directions, 1994.

———. *Landscape over Zero.* Trans. David Hinton. New York: New Directions, 1995.

———. *Notes from the City of the Sun.* Ed. and trans. Bonnie S. McDougall. Ithaca: China-Japan Program, Cornell University, 1984.

———. *Old Snow.* Trans. Bonnie S. McDougall and Chen Maiping. New York: New Directions, 1991.

———. *Wuren Shixuan.* Beijing: Zuojia Chubanshe, 1986.

Benedict, Ruth. *The Chrysanthemum and the Sword: Patterns of Japanese Culture.* New York: Houghton Mifflin, 1946.

———. *Patterns of Culture.* Boston: Houghton Mifflin, 1934.

Benjamin, Walter. *Illuminations.* Trans. Harry Zohn. New York: Schocken Books, 1969.

———. *Reflections.* Ed. Peter Demetz. Trans. Edmund Jephcott. New York: Schocken Books, 1978.

Berman, Antoine. *The Experience of the Foreign: Culture and Translation in Romantic Germany.* Trans. S. Heyvaert. Albany: State University of New York Press, 1992.

Bernstein, Charles. *My Way: Speeches and Poems.* Chicago: University of Chicago Press, 1999.

———. *A Poetics.* Cambridge: Harvard University Press, 1992.

———. "Stein's Identity." *Modern Fiction Studies* 42.3 (1996): 485–88.

———, ed. *The Politics of Poetic Form: Poetry and Public Policy.* New York: Roof Books, 1990.

Biggers, Earl Derr. *The Black Camel.* New York: Gross & Dunlap, 1929.

————. *Charlie Chan Carries On.* 1930. Reprint, New York: Pyramid Books, 1969.

————. *The Chinese Parrot.* New York: Gross & Dunlap, 1926.

————. *The House without a Key.* New York: Collier, 1925.

————. *Keeper of the Keys.* 1932. Reprint, New York: Bantam Books, 1975.

Bloom, Harold. "They Have the Numbers; We, the Heights." *Boston Review* 23.2 (April/May 1998): 24–29.

————. *The Western Canon: The Books and School of Ages.* New York: Harcourt Brace, 1994.

————, ed. *Asian American Women Writers.* Philadelphia: Chelsea House Publishers, 1997.

Boas, Franz, ed. *Handbook of American Indian Languages.* Washington: Government Printing Office, 1911.

————. *Race, Language, and Culture.* 1940. Reprint, Chicago: The University of Chicago Press, 1982.

Boodberg, Peter A. *Selected Works of Peter A. Boodberg.* Comp. Alvin P. Cohen. Berkeley and Los Angeles: University of California Press, 1979.

Brooks, Van Wyck. *Fenollosa and His Circle.* New York: E. P. Dutton, 1962.

Carpenter, Frederic Ives. *Emerson and Asia.* Cambridge: Harvard University Press, 1930.

Certeau, Michel de. *The Practice of Everyday Life.* Trans. Steven Rendall. Berkeley and Los Angeles: University of California Press, 1984.

Chan, Jeffery, et al., eds. *The Big Aiiieeeee! An Anthology of Chinese American and Japanese American Literature.* New York: Meridian, 1991.

Chang, Juliana. "Reading Asian American Poetry." *MELUS* 21.1 (1996): 81–98.

Chen, Xiaomei. *Occidentalism: A Theory of Counterdiscourse in Post-Mao China.* New York: Oxford University Press, 1995.

Cheung, King-Kok. *Articulate Silences: Hisaye Yamamoto, Maxine Hong Kingston, Joy Kogawa.* Ithaca: Cornell University Press, 1993.

Cheung, King-Kok, and Stan Yogi, eds. *Asian American Literature: An Annotated Bibliography.* New York: Modern Language Associations of America, 1988.

Chin, Frank. "Come All Ye Asian American Writers of the Real and the Fake." In *The Big Aiiieeeee! An Anthology of Chinese American and Japanese American Literature*, ed. Jeffery Chan, et al. New York: Meridian, 1991.

Chisolm, Lawrence. *Fenollosa: The Far East and American Culture.* New Haven: Yale University Press, 1963.

Chow, Rey. *Primitive Passions: Visuality, Sexuality, and Contemporary Chinese Cinema.* New York: Columbia University Press, 1995.

——. *Writing Diaspora: Tactics of Intervention in Contemporary Cultural Studies.* Bloomington: Indiana University Press, 1993.

Clifford, James. *The Predicament of Culture: Twentieth-Century Ethnography, Literature, and Art.* Cambridge: Harvard University Press, 1988.

——. *Routes: Travel and Translation in the Late Twentieth Century.* Cambridge: Harvard University Press, 1997.

Clifford, James, and George Marcus, eds. *Writing Culture: The Poetics and Politics of Ethnography.* Berkeley and Los Angeles: University of California Press, 1986.

Coffman, Stanley K., Jr. *Imagism: A Chapter for the History of Modern Poetry.* New York: Octagon Books, 1972.

Damon, S. Foster. *Amy Lowell: A Chronicle.* Hamden, Conn.: Archon Books, 1966.

Davenport, Guy. "Pound and Frobenius." In *Motives and Method in the Cantos of Ezra Pound,* ed. Lewis Leary. New York: Columbia University Press, 1954.

De Man, Paul. *Allegories of Reading.* New Haven: Yale University Press, 1979.

——. *The Resistance to Theory.* Minneapolis: University of Minnesota Press, 1986.

Derrida, Jacques. *Of Grammatology.* Trans. Gayatri Chakravorty Spivak. Baltimore: Johns Hopkins University Press, 1974.

Dirlik, Arif, ed. *What's In a Rim: Critical Perspectives on the Pacific Region Idea.* Boulder, Colo.: Westview Press, 1993.

Duo Duo. *Looking Out from Death: From the Cultural Revolution to Tiananmen Square.* Trans. Gregory Lee and John Cayley. London: Bloomsbury, 1989.

Eliot, T. S. "Introduction." *Ezra Pound: Selected Poems.* London: Faber and Faber, 1928.

Emerson, Ralph Waldo. *Essays and Lectures.* New York: Library of America, 1983.

Fabian, Johannes. *Time and the Other: How Anthropology Makes Its Object.* New York: Columbia University Press, 1983.

Fang, Achilles. "Fenollosa and Pound." *Harvard Journal of Asiatic Studies* 20 (1957): 213–38.

Fenollosa, Ernest. *The Chinese Written Character as a Medium for Poetry.* Ed. Ezra Pound. New York: Arrow Editions, 1936.

——. Editorial. *Golden Age* (June 1906).

——. *Epochs of Chinese and Japanese Art: An Outline History of East Asiatic Design.* New York: Stokes, 1900.

——. *Ernest F. Fenollosa's "Notes for a History of the Influence of China upon the Western World": A Link between the Houghton and the Beinecke Library Manuscripts.* Ed. Akiko Murakata. Kyoto, Japan: Kyoto University, 1982.

————. Unpublished notebooks. YCAL MSS 43, Box 98, Folder 4211 [B98 F4211] to Box 103, Folder 4282 [B103 F4282]. Beinecke Rare Book and Manuscript Library. New Haven: Yale University.

Finkel, Donald, and Carolyn Kizer. *A Splintered Mirror: Chinese Poetry from the Democracy Movement*. San Francisco: North Point Press, 1991.

Fisher, Philip, ed. *The New American Studies: Essays from* Representations. Berkeley and Los Angeles: University of California Press, 1991.

Foucault, Michel. *The Archaeology of Knowledge*. Trans. A. M. Sheridan Smith. New York: Pantheon Books, 1972.

Friedrich, Paul. *The Language Parallax: Linguistic Relativism and Poetic Indeterminacy*. Austin: University of Texas Press, 1986.

Frobenius, Leo. *The Childhood of Man: A Popular Account of the Lives, Customs & Thoughts of the Primitive Races*. Trans. A. H. Keane. London: Seeley, 1909.

Froula, Christine. *To Write Paradise: Style and Error in Pound's Cantos*. New Haven: Yale University Press, 1984.

Gadamer, Hans-Georg. *Truth and Method*. 2d, rev. ed. Trans. Joel Weinsheimer and Donald G. Marshall. New York: Continuum, 1995.

Gasché, Rodolphe. *Invention of Difference: On Jacques Derrida*. Cambridge: Harvard University Press, 1994.

————. *The Wild Card of Reading: On Paul de Man*. Cambridge: Harvard University Press, 1998.

Gates, Henry Louis, Jr. *The Signifying Monkey: A Theory of African-American Literary Criticism*. New York: Oxford University Press, 1988.

Geertz, Clifford. *The Interpretation of Cultures*. New York: BasicBooks, 1973.

————. *Works and Lives: The Anthropologist as Author*. Stanford: Stanford University Press, 1988.

Giles, Herbert A. *A History of Chinese Literature*. New York: D. Appleton, 1901.

Gilroy, Paul. *The Black Atlantic: Modernity and Double Consciousness*. Cambridge: Harvard University Press, 1993.

Gramsci, Antonio. *Selections from the Prison Notebooks*. Ed. and trans. Quintin Hoare and Geoffrey Nowell Smith. New York: International Publishers, 1971.

Greenblatt, Stephen J. *Learning to Curse: Essays in Early Modern Culture*. New York: Routledge, 1990.

————. *Marvelous Possessions: The Wonder of the New World*. Chicago: University of Chicago Press, 1991.

————. *Renaissance Self-Fashioning: From More to Shakespeare*. Chicago: University of Chicago Press, 1980.

Gu Cheng. *Selected Poems*. Ed. Sean Golden and Chu Chiyu. Hong Kong: Renditions, 1990.

Guillory, John. *Cultural Capital: The Problems of Literary Canon Formation*. Chicago: University of Chicago Press, 1993.

Hanke, Ken. *Charlie Chan at the Movies: History, Filmography and Criticism*. Jefferson, N.C.: Mcfarland, 1989.

Harmer, J. B. *Victory in Limbo: Imagism 1908–1917*. London: Secker & Warburg, 1975.

Hearn, Lafcadio. *Glimpses of Unfamiliar Japan*. Boston: Houghton Mifflin, 1894.

Hegel, Georg Wilhelm Friedrich. "Introduction to the Philosophy of Art." In *The Critical Tradition: Classic Texts and Contemporary Trends*, ed. David H. Richter. New York: St. Martin's Press, 1989.

Heidegger, Martin. *Being and Time*. Trans. John Macquarrie and Edward Robinson. New York: Harper and Row, 1962.

———. *Identity and Difference*. Trans. Joan Stambaugh. New York: Harper & Row, 1969.

Herder, Johann Gottfried von. *Outlines of a Philosophy of the History of Man*. Trans. T. Churchill. 1784. Reprint, New York: Bergman Publishers, 1966.

Herskovits, Melville J. *Franz Boas: The Science of Man in the Making*. New York: Charles Scribner's Sons, 1953.

Hobart, Alice Tisdale. *Within the Walls of Nanking*. London: Jonathan Cape, 1928.

Howe, Susan. *My Emily Dickinson*. Berkeley: North Atlantic Books, 1985.

Howland, D. R. *Borders of Chinese Civilization: Geography and History at Empire's End*. Durham: Duke University Press, 1996.

Huang, Yunte. *Shi: A Radical Reading of Chinese Poetry*. New York: Roof Books, 1997.

———. "The Translator's Invisible Hand: The Problems in the Introduction of Contemporary Chinese Poetry." *River City: A Journal of Contemporary Culture* 16.1 (1996): 68–81.

———. "Writing against the Chinese Diaspora." *boundary 2: An International Journal of Literature and Culture* 26.1 (1999): 145–46.

Hughes, Glenn. *Imagism and the Imagists: A Study in Modern Poetry*. New York: The Humanities Press, 1960.

Hurston, Zora Neale. *Mules and Men*. 1935. Reprint, New York: HarperPerennial, 1990.

Isaacs, Harold R. *Scratches on Our Minds: American Images of China and India*. New York: John Day, 1958.

Jahn, Janheinz. *Leo Frobenius: The Demonic Child*. Trans. Reinhard Sander. Austin:

African and Afro-American Studies and Research Center of the University of Texas, 1974.

Jakobson, Roman. *Language in Literature*. Cambridge: Harvard University Press, 1987.

James, Henry. *The Question of Our Speech*. Boston: Houghton Mifflin, 1905.

Jespersen, Otto. *Progress in Language*. London: Swan Sonnenschein, 1894.

Jinan Daxue Zhongwenxi, ed. *Zhongguo Lidai Shige Mingpian Shangxi*. Changsha, China: Hunan Renming Chubanshe, 1983.

Kenner, Hugh. *The Pound Era*. Berkeley and Los Angeles: University of California Press, 1971.

Kern, Robert. *Orientalism, Modernism, and the American Poem*. Cambridge: Cambridge University Press, 1996.

Kim, Elaine H. *Asian American Literature: An Introduction to the Writings and Their Social Context*. Philadelphia: Temple University Press, 1982.

Kingston, Maxine Hong. *China Men*. New York: Alfred A. Knopf, 1980.

———. "Cultural Mis-Reading by American Reviewers." In *Asian and Western Writers in Dialogue: New Cultural Identities*, ed. Guy Amirthanayagam. London: Macmillan, 1982.

———. *Tripmaster Monkey: His Fake Book*. New York: Vintage, 1990.

———. *The Woman Warrior: Memoirs of a Girlhood among Ghosts*. 1975. Reprint, New York: Vintage, 1989.

Kodama, Sanehide. *American Poetry and Japanese Culture*. Hamden, Conn.: Archon Books, 1984.

Kristeva, Julia. *The Kristeva Reader*. Ed. Toril Moi. New York: Columbia University Press, 1986.

———. *Revolution in Poetic Language*. Trans. Margaret Waller. New York: Columbia University Press, 1984.

Lach, Donald. *Asia in the Making of Europe*. Vol. 1, bk. 1. Chicago: University of Chicago Press, 1965.

Lears, T. J. Jackson. *No Place of Grace: Antimodernism and the Transformation of American Culture, 1880–1920*. Chicago: University of Chicago Press, 1994.

Lee, Robert G. *Orientals: Asian Americans in Popular Culture*. Philadelphia: Temple University Press, 1999.

Leibniz, Gottfried Wilhelm. *Writings on China*. Ed. and trans. Daniel J. Cook and Henry Rosemont Jr. Chicago: Open Court, 1994.

Lew, Walter, ed. *Premonitions: The Kaya Anthology of New Asian North American Poetry*. New York: Kaya Production, 1995.

Lim, Shirley Geok-lin. "Twelve Asian American Writers: In Search of Self-Definition." *MELUS* 13.1–2 (1986): 57–77.

Lim, Shirley Geok-lin, and Amy Ling, eds. *Reading Literatures of Asian America.* Philadelphia: Temple University Press, 1992.

Lin, Patricia. "Clashing Constructs of Reality: Reading Maxine Hong Kingston's *Tripmaster Monkey: His Fake Book* as Indigenous Ethnography." In *Reading Literatures of Asian America,* ed. Shirley Geok-Lin Lim and Amy Ling. Philadelphia: Temple University Press, 1992.

————. "The Icicle in the Desert: Perspective and Form in the Works of Two Chinese American Women Writers." *MELUS* 6.3 (1979): 51–71.

Lin Yutang. *The Little Critic: Essays, Satires and Sketches on China,* 2d series, 1933–35. Westport, Conn.: Hyperion Press, 1935.

————. *My Country and My People.* New York: John Day, 1935.

Lindberg, Kathryne V. *Reading Pound Reading: Modernism after Nietzsche.* New York: Oxford University Press, 1987.

Liu, Lydia H. *Translingual Practice: Literature, National Culture, and Translated Modernity—China, 1900–1937.* Stanford: Stanford University Press, 1995.

Lowe, Lisa. *Immigrant Acts: On Asian American Cultural Politics.* Durham: Duke University Press, 1996.

Lowell, Amy. *Can Grande's Castle.* New York: Macmillan, 1918.

————. *The Complete Poetical Works of Amy Lowell.* Boston: Houghton Mifflin, 1955.

————. *Fir-Flower Tablets: Poems from the Chinese.* Trans. Amy Lowell. Boston: Houghton Mifflin, 1921.

————. *Florence Ayscough and Amy Lowell: Correspondence of a Friendship.* Ed. Harley Farnsworth MacNair. Chicago: University of Chicago Press, 1945.

————. "An Observer in China." Review of *Profiles from China,* by Eunice Tietjens. *Poetry* 10 (September 1917): 326–30.

————. *Pictures of the Floating World.* New York: Macmillan, 1919.

Lowell, Percival. *Chosön: The Land of the Morning Calm.* Boston: Ticknor, 1886.

————. *Noto: An Unexplored Corner of Japan.* Boston: Houghton Mifflin, 1891.

————. *Occult Japan, or, The Way of the Gods: An Esoteric Study of Japanese Personality and Possession.* Boston: Houghton Mifflin, 1894.

————. *The Soul of the Far East.* New York: Macmillan, 1911.

Lowie, Robert H. *The History of Ethnological Theory.* New York: Rinehart, 1937.

Marcus, George, and Michael Fischer. *Anthropology as Cultural Critique: An Experimental Moment in the Human Sciences.* Chicago: University of Chicago Press, 1986.

Michaels, Walter Benn. "American Modernism and the Poetics of Identity." *MODERNISM/Modernity* 1.1 (1993): 38–56.

———. *Our America: Nativism, Pluralism and Modernism.* Durham: Duke University Press, 1997.

Miller, Owen. "Intertextual Identity." In *Identity of the Literary Text,* ed. Mario J. Valdés and Owen Miller. Toronto: University of Toronto Press, 1985.

Morin, Edward. *The Red Azalea: Chinese Poetry since the Cultural Revolution.* Honolulu: University of Hawaii Press, 1990.

Morse, Edward. *Japan Day by Day.* Vol. 1. Boston: Houghton Mifflin, 1917.

Mungello, David E. *Curious Land: Jesuit Accommodation and the Origins of Sinology.* Stuttgart, Germany: F. Steiner Verlag Wiesbaden, 1985.

Murakata, Akiko, ed. *Ernest F. Fenollosa's "Notes for a History of the Influence of China upon the Western World": A Link between the Houghton and the Beinecke Library Manuscripts.* Kyoto, Japan: Kyoto University, 1982.

Nicholls, Peter. *Modernisms: A Literary Guide.* Berkeley and Los Angeles: University of California Press, 1995.

North, Michael. *The Dialect of Modernism: Race, Language, and Twentieth-Century Literature.* New York: Oxford University Press, 1994.

Ong, Aihwa. *Flexible Citizenship: The Cultural Logics of Transnationality.* Durham: Duke University Press, 1999.

Ong, Aihwa, and Donald Nonini, eds. *Ungrounded Empires: The Cultural Politics of Modern Chinese Transnationalism.* New York: Routledge, 1997.

Owen, Stephen. "What Is World Poetry?" *New Republic* (November 19, 1990): 28–32.

Palumbo-Liu, David. *Asian/American: Historical Crossings of a Racial Frontier.* Stanford: Stanford University Press, 1999.

Pease, Donald, ed. *National Identities and Post-Americanist Narratives.* Durham: Duke University Press, 1994.

———, ed. *Revisionary Interventions into the Americanist Canon.* Durham: Duke University Press, 1994.

Perloff, Marjorie. *The Dance of the Intellect: Studies in the Poetry of the Pound Tradition.* 1985. Reprint, Evanston, Ill.: Northwestern University Press, 1996.

———. "Modernism without the Modernists: A Response to Walter Benn Michaels." *MODERNISM/Modernity* 3.1 (1996): 99–105.

———. Review of *Forbidden Entries,* by John Yau. *Boston Review* 22.3–4 (1997): 39–41.

———. "Visionary Company." *Boston Review* 23.3–4 (1998): 23.

———. *Wittgenstein's Ladder: Poetic Language and the Strangeness of the Ordinary.* Chicago: University of Chicago Press, 1996.

Polo, Marco. *The Book of Marco Polo, the Venetian: Concerning the Kingdoms and Marvels of the East.* Trans. and ed. Colonel Henry Yule. London: John Murray, 1871.

Pound, Ezra. *The Cantos of Ezra Pound.* New York: New Directions, 1972.

———. *Cathay.* London: Elkin Mathews, 1915.

———. *The Classic Anthology Defined by Confucius.* Cambridge: Harvard University Press, 1954.

———. *Ezra Pound: Selected Poems.* Ed. T. S. Eliot. London: Faber and Faber, 1928.

———. *Guide to Kulchur.* New York: New Directions, 1938.

———. *Literary Essays of Ezra Pound.* Ed. T. S. Eliot. London: Faber and Faber, 1954.

———. *Personae.* New York: New Directions, 1990.

———. *Selected Prose.* Ed. William Cookson. London: Faber and Faber, 1973.

———. "Vorticism." *Fortnightly Review* n.s. 96 (July-Sep. 1914): 461–71.

———, ed. *The Chinese Written Character as a Medium for Poetry*, by Ernest Fenollosa. New York: Arrows Editions, 1936.

———, ed. *Des Imagistes.* New York: Albert and Charles Boni, 1914.

Pratt, Mary Louise. "Fieldwork in Common Places." In *Writing Culture: The Poetics and Politics of Ethnography*, ed. James Clifford and George Marcus. Berkeley and Los Angeles: University of California Press, 1986.

———. *Imperial Eyes: Travel Writing and Transculturation.* London: Routledge, 1992.

Qian, Zhaoming. *Orientalism and Modernism.* Durham: Duke University Press, 1995.

Quartermain, Peter. *Disjunctive Poetics: From Gertrude Stein and Louis Zukofsky to Susan Howe.* Cambridge: Cambridge University Press, 1992.

Radin, Paul. *The Culture of the Winnebago: As Described by Themselves.* Bloomington, Ind.: Special publications of Bollingen Foundation, no. 1, 1947.

Raz, Hilda. Editorial. *Prairie Schooner* 65. 2 (1991): 4.

Ricoeur, Paul. *Hermeneutics and the Human Sciences.* Ed. and trans. John B. Thompson. Cambridge: Cambridge University Press, 1981.

———. *Interpretation Theory: Discourse and the Surplus of Meaning.* Fort Worth: Texas Christian University Press, 1976.

———. "The Text as Dynamic Identity." In *Identity of the Literary Text*, ed. Mario J. Valdés and Owen Miller. Toronto: University of Toronto Press, 1985.

Riffaterre, Michael. "The Making of the Text." In *Identity of the Literary Text*, ed. Mario J. Valdés and Owen Miller. Toronto: University of Toronto Press, 1985.

Rohmer, Sax. *The Insidious Dr. Fu-Manchu*. New York: McBride, Nast, 1913.

———. *The Mystery of Dr. Fu-Manchu*. London: Methuen, 1913.

Rowe, John Carlos. *Literary Culture and U.S. Imperialism: From the Revolution to World War II*. New York: Oxford University Press, 2000.

Said, Edward. *Orientalism*. New York: Vintage Books, 1979.

Sakai, Naoki. *Translation and Subjectivity: On "Japan" and Cultural Nationalism*. Minneapolis: University of Minnesota Press, 1997.

———. *Voices of the Past: The Status of Language in Eighteenth-Century Japanese Discourse*. Ithaca: Cornell University Press, 1991.

Saldívar, José David. *Border Matters: Remapping American Cultural Studies*. Berkeley and Los Angeles: University of California Press, 1997.

Sapir, Edward. *Selected Writings of Edward Sapir in Language, Culture and Society*. Ed. D. G. Mandelbaum. Berkeley and Los Angeles: University of California Press, 1949.

Searle, John R. *Speech Acts: An Essay in the Philosophy of Language*. Cambridge: Cambridge University Press, 1969.

Sollors, Werner. *Beyond Ethnicity: Consent and Descent in American Culture*. New York: Oxford University Press, 1986.

———, ed. *Multilingual America: Transnationalism, Ethnicity, and the Languages of American Literature*. New York: New York University Press, 1998.

Sollors, Werner, and Marc Shell, eds. *Multilingual Anthology of American Literature*. New York: New York University Press, 2000.

Soong, Stephen, and John Minford. *Trees on the Mountain: An Anthology of New Chinese Writing*. Seattle: University of Washington Press, 1984.

Spence, Jonathan. *The Chan's Great Continent: China in Western Minds*. New York: W. W. Norton, 1998.

Stein, Gertrude. *The Making of Americans: Being a History of a Family's Progress*. 1925. Reprint, Normal, Ill.: Dalkey Archive Press, 1995.

———. *A Stein Reader*. Ed. Ulla E. Dydo. Evanston: Northwestern University Press, 1993.

Strassberg, Richard E. *Inscribed Landscape: Travel Writing from Imperial China*. Berkeley and Los Angeles: University of California Press, 1994.

Tanaka, Stefan. *Japan's Orient: Rendering Pasts into History*. Berkeley and Los Angeles: University of California Press, 1993.

Tedlock, Dennis. *The Spoken Word and the Work of Interpretation*. Philadelphia: University of Pennsylvania Press, 1983.

Tedlock, Dennis, and Bruce Mannheim, eds. *The Dialogic Emergence of Culture*. Urbana: University of Illinois Press, 1995.

Tietjens, Eunice. *Profiles from China*. Chicago: Ralph Fletcher Seymour, 1917.

Toler, Sidney. *Stage Fright and Other Verses*. Portland: Smith and Sale, 1910.

Twitchell, Jeffrey. "Chinese Poetic Postmodernism? Introduction to the Original Poets." *Polygraph* 5 (1992): 221–34.

———. "Original: Chinese Language-Poetry Group." In *Exact Change Yearbook*, no. 1. Boston: Exact Change, 1995.

Valdés, Mario J., and Owen Miller, eds. *Identity of the Literary Text*. Toronto: University of Toronto Press, 1985.

Venuti, Lawrence. *The Translator's Invisibility: A History of Translation*. New York: Routledge, 1995.

Versluis, Arthur. *American Transcendentalism and Asian Religions*. New York: Oxford University Press, 1993.

Wang, Ping. *The New Generation: Poems from China Today*. New York: Hanging Loose Press, 1999.

Williams, Raymond. *Keywords: A Vocabulary of Culture and Society*. New York: Oxford University Press, 1976.

Wilson, Rob. *Reimagining the American Pacific: From South Pacific to Bamboo Ridge and Beyond*. Durham: Duke University Press, 2000.

Wilson, Rob, and Arif Dirlik, eds. *Asia/Pacific as Space of Cultural Production*. Durham: Duke University Press, 1995.

Wittgenstein, Ludwig. *Lectures and Conversations on Aesthetics, Psychology, and Religious Belief*. Ed. Cyril Barrett. Berkeley and Los Angles: University of California Press, 1996.

———. *Philosophical Investigations*. Trans. G. E. M. Anscombe. New York: Macmillan, 1958.

Wolfe, Cary. *The Limits of American Literary Ideology in Pound and Emerson*. New York: Cambridge University Press, 1993.

Wong, Sau-ling Cynthia. "Necessity and Extravagance in Maxine Hong Kingston's *The Woman Warrior*." *MELUS* 15.1 (1988): 4–26.

———. *Reading Asian American Literature: From Necessity to Extravagance*. Princeton: Princeton University Press, 1993.

Wu, Qing-yun. "A Chinese Reader's Response to Maxine Hong Kingston's *China Men*." *MELUS* 17.3 (1991–92): 85–94.

Yang Lian. *Masks and Crocodile*. Trans. Mabel Lee. Sydney, Australia: Wild Peony, 1990.

Yau, John. *Edificio Sayonara*. Santa Rosa, Calif.: Black Sparrow Press, 1989.

———. *Forbidden Entries*. Santa Rosa, Calif.: Black Sparrow Press, 1996.

———. "Interview with Edward Foster." *Talisman* 5 (1990): 31–50.

———. *Sometimes*. New York: The Sheep Meadow Press, 1979.

Yeh, Michelle. *Anthology of Modern Chinese Poetry*. New Haven: Yale University Press, 1992.

Yin, Xiao-huang. "Worlds of Difference: Lin Yutang, Lao She, and the Significance of Chinese-Language Writing in America." In *Multilingual America: Transnationalism, Ethnicity, and the Languages of American Literature*, ed. Werner Sollors. New York: New York University Press, 1998.

Yip, Wai-Lim. *Ezra Pound's Cathay*. Princeton: Princeton University Press, 1969.

Yu, Beongcheon. *The Great Circle: American Writers and the Orient*. Detroit: Wayne State University Press, 1983.

Zhang, Longxi. *The Tao and the Logos: Literary Hermeneutics, East and West*. Durham: Duke University Press, 1992.

Zhu, Guangqian. *Shilun* (On poetry). Beijing: Sanlian Shudian, 1985.

INDEX

Composition:	Impressions Book and Journal Services, Inc.
Text:	10/15 Janson
Display:	Janson
Printer:	Sheridan Books, Inc.
Binder:	Sheridan Books, Inc.